Junior Poetry Workshop

NEW EDITION

Edited by

N. RUSSELL

and

H.J. CHATFIELD

Illustrated by

Inga Moor

NELSON

Nelson I(T)P®
102 Dodds Street
South Melbourne 3205

Nelson I(T)P® *an International Thomson Publishing company*

First published in Australia 1966
Reprinted 8 times

New edition published 1977
25 24 23 22 21 20 19 18
05 04 03 02 01 00 99 98

ISBN 0 17 005181 1

Printed in Hong Kong

Preface

Here is a new *Junior Poetry Workshop.*

Those familiar with the first edition will notice many changes. The new poems we have introduced and the old favourites we have retained will, we hope, be enjoyed by the pupils in junior forms of secondary schools. They will find stories to involve them, situations and people to laugh at and verses and ballads to read, sing and act. The more challenging poems will help them appreciate the craftsmanship of the poet and deepen their awareness of themselves and others.

If the selections and activities encourage boys and girls to find pleasure in reading poetry and satisfaction from their discussion and writing, the 'workshop' will have achieved its aim.

H. J. C.
N. R.

Contents

3 Cats and Dogs

4 People

5 Reading Aloud

6 Fun and Nonsense

7 Picture Writing

8   Feelings and Experiences

1 Violence

The Fear

A lantern light from deeper in the barn
Shone on a man and woman in the door
And threw their lurching shadows on a house
Nearby, all dark in every glossy window.
A horse's hoof pawed once the hollow floor,
And the back of the gig they stood beside
Moved in a little. The man grasped a wheel,
The woman spoke out sharply, ' Whoa, stand still!
I saw it just as plain as a white plate,'
She said, 'as the light on the dashboard ran
Along the bushes at the roadside – a man's face.
You *must* have seen it too.'

                              'I didn't see it.
Are you sure –'

              'Yes, I'm sure!'

                              '– it was a face?'
'Joel, I'll have to look. I can't go in,
I can't, and leave a thing like that unsettled.
Doors locked and curtains drawn will make no difference.
I always have felt strange when we came home
To the dark house after so long an absence,
And the key rattled loudly into place
Seemed to warn someone to be getting out
At one door as we entered at another.
What if I'm right, and someone all the time –
Don't hold my arm!'

'I say it's someone passing.'

'You speak as if this were a travelled road.
You forget where we are. What is beyond
That he'd be going to or coming from
At such an hour of night, and on foot too?
What was he standing still for in the bushes?

'It's not so very late – it's only dark.
There's more in it than you're inclined to say.
Did he look like – ?'

              'He looked like anyone.
I'll never rest tonight unless I know.
Give me the lantern.'

                    'You don't want the lantern.'

She pushed past him and got it for herself.

'You're not to come,' she said. 'This is my business
If the time's come to face it, I'm the one
To put it the right way. He'd never dare –
Listen! He kicked a stone. Hear that, hear that!
He's coming towards us. Joel, *go* in – please.
Hark! – I don't hear him now. But please go in.'

'In the first place you can't make me believe it's –'

'It is – or someone else he's sent to watch.
And now's the time to have it out with him
While we know definitely where he is.
Let him get off and he'll be everywhere
Around us, looking out of trees and bushes
Till I sha'n't dare to set a foot outdoors.
And I can't stand it. Joel, let me go!'

'But it's nonsense to think he'd care enough.'

'You mean you couldn't understand his caring.
Oh, but you see he hadn't had enough –
Joel, I won't – I won't – I promise you.
We mustn't say hard things. You mustn't either.'

'I'll be the one, if anybody goes!
But you give him the advantage with this light.
What couldn't he do to us standing here!
And if to see was what he wanted, why,
He has seen all there was to see and gone.'

He appeared to forget to keep his hold,
But advanced with her as she crossed the grass.

'What do you want?' she cried to all the dark.
She stretched up tall to overlook the light
That hung in both hands hot against her skirt.

'There's no one; so you're wrong,' he said.

                              'There is. –
What do you want?' she cried, and then herself
Was startled when an answer really came.

'Nothing.' It came from well along the road.

She reached out a hand to Joel for support:
The smell of scorching woollen made her faint.
'What are you doing round this house at night?'

'Nothing.' A pause: there seemed no more to say.

And then the voice again: 'You seem afraid.
I saw by the way you whipped up the horse.
I'll just come forward in the lantern light
And let you see.'

                    'Yes, do. – Joel, go back!'

She stood her ground against the noisy steps
That came on, but her body rocked a little.

'You see,' the voice said.
                    'Oh.' She looked and looked.

'You don't see – I've a child here by the hand.
A robber wouldn't have his family with him.'

'What's a child doing at this time of night – ?'

'Out walking. Every child should have the memory
Of at least one long-after-bedtime walk.
What, son?'

'Then I should think you'd try to find
Somewhere to walk –'

                    'The highway, as it happens –
We're stopping for the fortnight down at Dean's.'
'But if that's all – Joel – you realize –
You won't think anything. You understand?
You understand that we have to be careful.
This is a very, very lonely place.
Joel!' She spoke as if she couldn't turn.
The swinging lantern lengthened to the ground,
It touched, it struck, it clattered and went out.

                                        Robert Frost

---

*The readers of this poem are kept in suspense as the fear and tension
of Joel and his wife mount. What are some of the most spine-chilling
moments? How has Robert Frost made you feel as if you were actually
experiencing the fear?*

*The lantern 'clattered and went out'. Continue the story from that
point.*

*Discuss the fears that have caused your own heart to thump. Try
to convey the terror to your listeners.*

The Fifth Sense

'*A 65-year-old Cypriot Greek shepherd, Nicolis Loizon, was wounded by security forces early today. He was challenged twice; when he failed to answer, troops opened fire. A subsequent hospital examination showed that the man was deaf.*'

NEWS ITEM, 30 December 1957

Lamps burn all the night
Here, where people must be watched and seen,
And I, a shepherd, Nicolis Loizon,
Wish for the dark, for I have been
Sure-footed in the dark, but now my sight
Stumbles among these beds, scattered white boulders,
As I lean towards my far slumbering house
With the night lying upon my shoulders.

My sight was always good,
Better than others. I could taste wine and bread
And name the field they spattered when the harvest
Broke. I could coil in the red
Scent of the fox out of a maze of wood
And grass. I could touch mist, I could touch breath.
But of my sharp senses I had only four.
The fifth one pinned me to my death.

The soldiers must have called
The word they needed: Halt. Not hearing it,
I was their failure, relaxed against the winter
Sky, the flag of their defeat.
With their five senses they could not have told
That I lacked one, and so they had to shoot.
They would fire at a rainbow if it had
A colour less than they were taught,

Christ said that when one sheep
Was lost, the rest meant nothing any more.
Here in this hospital, where others' breathing
Swings like a lantern in the polished floor
And squeezes those who cannot sleep,
I see how precious each thing is, how dear,
For I may never touch, smell, taste, or see
Again, because I could not hear.

Patricia Beer

*Patricia Beer has thought about a bald news item in the daily paper.
Her perception and imagination have re-created the scene for us and
have enabled us to enter the mind of the Greek shepherd.*

*Read the following news item and see whether you can, in the same
way, bring the incident alive in a story or a poem.*

*A bushman today discovered the wreckage of the DC7 plane missing
since April 7. Only two passengers, a 10 year old boy and a girl of
7, were found. That anyone should survive 9 days in such dense
rain forest is nothing less than miraculous.*

News Item, 15 April 1974

The Fugitive

That ditch of rushes, is it deep
Enough for me to creep
And hide there, till the pursuing horsemen pass?
The osier, will it droop
And cloak me, while the troop
Thuds o'er the miry track among the grass?

My scarf of crimson I have thrown
Into a puddle brown;
They will catch no glint of red beneath the trees;
I may escape their eyes,
But these wild breaths that rise
And buffet me, hearkening they might hear these!

Spur rascals, that your clattering din
May drown all else therein,
That I may gasp and sob unheard of you!
Spur – for if ye draw rein
I shall not see again
The meadows pranked with pearls of morning dew.

The dew of dusk will glimmer soon
And the derisive moon
Look down – on what? – They pass! Their thundering
    rush
Knocks louder on my ear;
Nay, 'tis my heart I hear –
They have drawn rein to listen. One said '*Hush*!'

Dorothy Stuart

*Dorothy Stuart has so sensitively created the predicament of the hunted
man that you are able to share his feelings of fearful suspense.
    Questions throng to your mind as you read the poem:*

to what period of history does the incident belong?
why is the fugitive being hunted to death?
why is he on foot and the others mounted?
is he the evil-doer or are his foes bad men?
did he escape or ...?

The Death of Ned Kelly

Ned Kelly fought the rich men in country and in town,
Ned Kelly fought the troopers until they ran him down;
He thought that he had fooled them, for he was hard to find,
But he rode into Glenrowan with the troopers close behind.

'Come out of that, Ned Kelly,' the head zarucker calls,
'Come out and leave your shelter, or we'll shoot it full of
    holes.'
'If you take *me*,' says Kelly, 'that's not the speech to use;
I've lived to spite your order, I'll die the way I choose!'

'Come out of that, Ned Kelly, you done a lawless thing:
You robbed and fought the squatters, Ned Kelly, you must
    swing.'
'If those who rob,' says Kelly, 'are all condemned to die,
You had better hang the squatters; they've stolen more
    than I.'

'You'd best come out, Ned Kelly, you done the government
    wrong,
For you held up the coaches that bring the gold along.'
'Go tell your boss,' says Kelly, 'who lets the rich go free,
That your bloody rich man's government will never govern
    me.'

'You talk all right, Ned Kelly, your tongue is slick, I own;
But I have men to help me and you are all alone.'
They burned the roof above him, they fired the walls about,
And head to foot in armour Ned Kelly stumbled out.

Although his guns were empty he took them by surprise;
He wore an iron breastplate and armour on his thighs.
Although his guns were empty he made them turn and flee,
But one came in behind him and shot him in the knee.

And so they took Ned Kelly and hanged him in the jail,
For he fought singlehanded although in iron mail.
And no man singlehanded can hope to break the bars;
It's a thousand like Ned Kelly who'll hoist the Flag of Stars.

John Manifold

The Road To Roma Jail

It's a long road, a cruel road, the road to Roma jail,
  Birds in all the branches mocking as you pass,
  The spiteful little soldier-bird, the stupid old jackass,
Crying, 'One, two, three of them; riding head to tail,'
On the long road, the cruel road, the road to Roma jail.

Crookedly the track runs beneath the grassy skies,
  Silver shines the mulga, golden glows the plain,
  Bullocks in the barley-grass start and stare again,
Stockmen at the station-yards watch the white dust rise,
But one man, jogging on, dare not raise his eyes.

Pride of life and wild blood, all must pay the toll,
  Stolen horses' mouths are hard as misers' hearts,
  None know where the end is once the journey starts,
And Steve rides a long ride to reach a bitter goal,
While black imps, grinning imps, hover round his soul.

It's a long road, a cruel road, the road to Roma jail,
  A trooper rides behind you, a tracker rides before,
  Your hands are tied, your head bowed, your heart and
    body sore,
And high above you in the blue the homing wood-duck
  sail,
On the long road, the cruel road, the road to Roma jail.

Vance Palmer

Put yourself in the place of Steve. Write a letter from Roma Jail to your young brother, describing the incident that led to your capture. (If you read the opening pages of Rolf Boldrewood's Robbery Under Arms you will find a prose description of a similar situation.)

In the poems about outlaws, find evidence suggesting that the poets have made us pity and even admire the law-breakers.

Discuss in class: Should Australians glorify bushrangers and lawbreakers as heroes?

Find a recording of the ballad 'The Streets of Laredo'. A group might learn the ballad and present it to guitar accompaniment.

The Streets of Laredo

As I walked out in the streets of Laredo,
As I walked out in Laredo one day,
I spied a poor cowboy wrapped up in white linen,
Wrapped up in white linen as cold as the clay.

'I see by your outfit that you are a cowboy,'
These words he did say as I boldly stepped by.
'Come, sit down beside me and hear my sad story;
I was shot in the breast and I know I must die.

Once in my saddle I used to look handsome,
Once in my saddle I used to look gay.
I first went to drinkin' and then to card playin',
Got shot in the breast, which ended my day.

Let sixteen gamblers come handle my coffin,
Let sixteen girls come carry my pall;
Put bunches of roses all over my coffin,
Put roses to deaden the clods as they fall.

And beat the drums slowly and play the fife lowly,
And play the dead march as you carry me along;
Take me to the prairie and lay the sod o'er me,
For I'm a young cowboy and I know I've done wrong.'

We beat the drums slowly and played the fife lowly,
And bitterly wept as we bore him along;
For we all loved our comrade so brave, young and handsome,
We loved the young cowboy although he'd done wrong.

Anon.

Charley Lee

A low moon shone on the desert land and the sage was
    silver white,
As Lee – a thong round hand and hand – stood straight in
    the lantern light.
'You have strung up Red and Burke,' said he,
'And you say that the next will be Charley Lee,
But there's never a rope was made for me.'
And he laughed in the quiet night.

They shaped the noose and they flicked the rope and over
    the limb it fell,
And Charley Lee saw the ghost of hope go glimmering
    down to hell.
Two shadows swung from the cottonwood tree,
And the wind went whispering, 'Charley Lee,'
For the turning shadows would soon be three,
And never a stone to tell.

'Have ye more to say for yourself?' said Gray, 'A message
    the like, or prayer?
If ye have, then hasten and have your say. We trailed and
    we trapped ye fair,
With fire and iron at Hidden Sink,
Where none but the stolen horses drink,
And the chain but wanted a final link,
Ye were riding my red roan mare.'

'But prove your property first,' said Lee. 'Would you call
    the mare your own,
With never a brand or mark to see, or name to the big red
    roan?
But strip the saddle and turn her loose,
And I'll show that the mare is my own cayuse.
And I don't – then take it a fair excuse,
  To tighten the rope you've thrown.'

Gaunt, grim faces and steady eyes were touched with a
    sombre look,
And hands slipped slowly to belted thighs and held on a
    finger-crook,
For Gray of Mesa who claimed the mare,
Had talked too much as he led them there,
Nor other among them knew the lair,
So a grip on their haste they took.

'Give him a chance,' said Monty Wade, and 'What is the
    use?' said Blake,
'He's done,' said Harney; 'his string is played. But we'll give
    him an even break.'
So they led the mare to the cottonwood tree,
Nor saddle nor bridle nor rope had she.
'Bonnie, come here!' said Charley Lee,
And soft was the word he spake.

The roan mare came and she nosed his side and nuzzled him
     friendly wise;
'Kneel!' cried Lee, and he leaped astride and fled as the
     swallow flies.
Flashes followed his flight in vain,
Bullets spattered the ground like rain,
Hoofs drummed far on the midnight plain,
And a low moon rode the skies.

Dawn broke red on the desert land where the turning
    shadows fell,
And the wind drove over the rolling sand with a whimpering
    ebb and swell,
Whimpering, whispering, 'Charley Lee,'
As south on the red roan mare rode he,
Yet the turning shadows they were three,
And never a stone to tell.

Henry Herbert Knibbs

'*Charley Lee*' *is a dramatic story in verse. Arrange it for presentation
to the class, with parts for a narrator, Charley Lee, Gray, Wade,
Blake and Harney.*

    *Solve this puzzle: In the second stanza we read that '*the turning
shadows would soon be three*' when Charley Lee was hanged alongside
the bodies of Red and Burke. In the last stanza we are told that '*the
turning shadows they were three*', although we know that Lee escaped.
Account for the third shadow.*

The Tarry Buccaneer

I'm going to be a pirate with a bright brass pivot-gun,
And an island in the Spanish Main beyond the setting sun,
And a silver flagon of red wine to drink when work is done,
    Like a fine old salt-sea scavenger, like a tarry Buccaneer.

With a sandy creek to careen in, and a pig-tailed Spanish
    Mate,
And under my main-hatches a sparkling merry freight
Of doubloons and double moidores and pieces of eight,
    Like a fine old salt-sea scavenger, like a tarry Buccaneer.

With a taste for Spanish wine-shops and for spending my
    doubloons,
And a crew of swart mulattoes and black-eyed octoroons,
And a thoughtful way with mutineers of making them
    maroons,
    Like a fine old salt-sea scavenger, like a tarry Buccaneer.

With a sash of crimson velvet and a diamond-hilted sword,
And a silver whistle about my neck secured to a golden cord,
And a habit of taking captives and walking them along a
    board,
    Like a fine old salt-sea scavenger, like a tarry Buccaneer.

With a spy-glass tucked beneath my arm and a cocked hat
    cocked askew,
And a long low rakish schooner a-cutting of the waves in
    two,
And a flag of skull and cross-bones the wickedest that ever
    flew,
    Like a fine old salt-sea scavenger, like a tarry Buccaneer.

John Masefield

*The boy has a romantic view of pirates. If you read about buccaneers
in history you may get a very different impression. Read, also, Chapter 3
of* Treasure Island *by R. L. Stevenson and see what a contrast the
blind pirate Pugh is to the buccaneer imagined by Masefield's boy.*

A Ballad of John Silver

We were schooner-rigged and rakish,
with a long and lissome hull,
And we flew the pretty
colours of the cross-
bones and the
skull;

We'd a big black Jolly Roger flapping grimly at the fore,
And we sailed the Spanish Water in the happy days of yore.

We'd a long brass gun amidships, like a well-conducted ship,
We had each a brace of pistols and a cutlass at the hip;
It's a point which tells against us, and a fact to be deplored,
But we chased the goodly merchant-men and laid their ships
    aboard.

Then the dead men fouled the scuppers and the wounded
    filled the chains,
And the paint-work all was spatter-dashed with other
    people's brains,
She was boarded, she was looted, she was scuttled till she
    sank.
And the pale survivors left us by the medium of the plank.

O! then it was (while standing by the taffrail on the poop)
We could hear the drowning folk lament the absent chicken-
    coop;
Then, having washed the blood away, we'd little else to do
Than to dance a quiet hornpipe as the old salts taught us to.

O! the fiddle on the fo'c'sle, and the slapping naked soles,
And the genial 'Down the middle, Jake, and curtsey when
    she rolls!'
With the silver seas around us and the pale moon overhead,
And the look-out not a-looking and his pipe-bowl glowing
    red.

Ah! the pig-tailed, quidding pirates and the pretty pranks
    we played,
All have since been put a stop-to by the naughty Board of
    Trade;
The schooners and the merry crews are laid away to rest,
A little south the sunset in the Islands of the Blest.

                                            John Masefield

Spanish Waters

Spanish waters, Spanish waters, you are ringing in my ears,
Like a slow sweet piece of music from the grey forgotten
years;
Telling tales, and beating tunes, and bringing weary thoughts
to me
Of the sandy beach at Muertos, where I would that I could
be.
We anchored at Los Muertos when the dipping sun was
red,
We left her half-a-mile to sea, to west of Nigger Head;
And before the mist was on the Cay, before the day was
done,
We were all ashore on Muertos with the gold that we had
won.
There's surf breaks on Los Muertos, and it never stops
to roar,
And it's there we came to anchor, and it's there we went
ashore,
Where the blue lagoon is silent amid snags of rotting trees,
Dropping like the clothes of corpses cast up by the seas.
We bore it through the marshes in a half-score battered
chests,
Sinking, in the sucking quagmires, to the sunburn on our
breasts.
Heaving over tree-trunks, gasping, damning at the flies and
heat,
Longing for a long drink, out of silver, in the ship's cool
lazareet.
The moon came white and ghostly as we laid the treasure
down,
There was gear there'd make a beggarman as rich as Lima
Town,
Copper charms and silver trinkets from the chests of
Spanish crews,
Gold doubloons and double moidores, louis d'ors and
portagues,

Clumsy yellow-metal earrings from the Indians of Brazil,
Uncut emeralds out of Rio, bezoar stones from Guayaquil;
Silver, in the crude and fashioned, pots of old Arica bronze,
Jewels from the bones of Incas desecrated by the Dons.
We smoothed the place with mattocks, and we took and
    blazed the tree,
Which marks yon where the gear is hid that none will ever
    see,
And we laid aboard the ship again, and south away we
    steers,
Through the loud surf of Los Muertos which is beating in
    my ears.

I'm the last alive that knows it. All the rest have gone their
    ways,
Killed, or died, or come to anchor in the old Mulatas Cays,
And I go singing, fiddling, old and starved and in despair,
And I know where all that gold is hid, if I were only there.

It's not the way to end it all. I'm old, and nearly blind,
And an old man's past's a strange thing, for it never leaves
    his mind.
And I see in dreams, awhiles, the beach, the sun's disc
    dipping red,
And the tall ship, under topsails, swaying in past Nigger
    Head.

I'd be glad to step ashore there. Glad to take a pick and go
To the lone blazed coco-palm tree in the place no others
    know,
And lift the gold and silver that has mouldered there for
    years
By the loud surf of Los Muertos which is beating in my
    ears.

John Masefield

*Imagine that the old blind pirate dies, and among his few possessions
is one clue to the whereabouts of the buried treasure. Write the story
that follows.*

On the Way to the Mission

They dogged him all one afternoon
Through the bright snow,
Two white men, servants of greed;
He knew that they were there,
But he turned not his head;
He was an Indian trapper;
He planted his snow-shoes firmly,
He dragged the long toboggan
Without rest.

The three figures drifted
Like shadows in the mind of a seer;
The snow-shoes were the whisperers
On the threshold of awe;
The toboggan made the sound of wings,
A wood pigeon sloping to her nest.

The Indian's face was calm.
He strode with the sorrow of fore-knowledge,
But his eyes were jewels of content
Set in circles of peace.

They would have shot him;
But momently in the deep forest,
They saw something flit by his side:
Their hearts stopped with fear.
Then the moon rose.
They would have left him to the spirit,
But they saw the long toboggan
Rounded well with furs,
With many a silver fox-skin,
With the pelts of mink and of otter,
They were the servants of greed;
When the moon grew brighter
And the spruces were dark with sleet,
They shot him.
When he fell on a shield of moonlight
One of his arms clung to his burden;
The snow was not melted:
The spirit passed away.

Then the servants of greed
Tore off the cover to count their gains;
They shuddered away into the shadows,
Hearing each the loud heart of the other.
Silence was born.

There in the tender moonlight,
    As sweet as they were in life,
Glimmered the ivory features
    Of the Indian's wife.

In the manner of Montagnais women
    Her hair was rolled with braid;

Under her waxen fingers
  A crucifix was laid.

He was drawing her down to the Mission,
  To bury her there in the spring,
When the bloodroot comes and the windflower
  To silver everything.

But as a gift of plunder
  Side by side were they laid,
The moon went on with her setting
  And covered them with shade.

                                        D. C. Scott

Two white men, a Red Indian of the Montagnais tribe, a toboggan covered with furs: out of this material the poet has made a drama of treachery and murder.

The first part of the poem is in free verse; the latter has regular stanzas, rhythm and rhyme. Can you find where the change comes, and suggest why the poet made the changes?

Imagine that the murderers did not go scot free. Perhaps the white man's law punished them; perhaps the Montagnais braves had revenge; perhaps the murderers' own panic destroyed them. Can you suggest other possibilities?

2 Witches and Ghosts

In olden days, Cornish folk used to say this prayer before they blew out their candles and snuggled down into bed. They believed in the powers of darkness – in the evil spirits who inhabited the mysterious world of the supernatural.

From Witches, Warlocks and Wurricoes,
From Ghoulies, Ghosties and Long-leggity beasties,
From all things that go BUMP in the night –
Good Lord deliver us!

'The Ride-by-Nights' is an enjoyable poem to read aloud. Notice the movements and sounds of the witches, and in your reading make them swoop and hover, swing and wheel as they chase each other pell-mell through the empty air.

The Ride-by-Nights

Up on their brooms the Witches stream,
Crooked and black in the crescent's gleam;
One foot high, and one foot low,
Bearded, cloaked, and cowled, they go.
'Neath Charlie's Wane they twitter and tweet,
And away they swarm 'neath the Dragon's feet,
With a whoop and a flutter they swing and sway,
And surge pell-mell down the Milky Way.
Between the legs of the glittering Chair
They hover and squeak in the empty air.
Then round they swoop past the glimmering Lion
To where Sirius barks behind huge Orion;
Up, then, and over to wheel amain
Under the silver, and home again.

Walter de la Mare

The Witch's Song

'Hoity-Toity! Hop-o'-my-Thumb!
Tweedledee and Tweedledum!
All hobgoblins come to me,
Over the mountains, over the sea;
Come in a hurry, come in a crowd,
Flying, chattering, shrieking loud;
I and my broomstick fidget and call –
Come, hobgoblins, we want you all!

'I have a pot of a mischievous brew;
You must do what I tell you to:
Blow through the keyholes, hang to the eaves,
Litter the garden with dead brown leaves;
Into the houses hustle and run,
Here is mischief and here is fun!
Break the china and slam the doors,
Crack the windows and scratch the floors,
Let in the cockroaches, mice and rats,
Sit on the family's Sunday hats;
Hiding and stealing everything little,
Smashing everything thin and brittle:
Teasing the children, tickling their heels –
Look at them jumping! Hark to their squeals!
Pinch their elbows and pull their hair,
Then out again to the gusty air!

'Flutter the birds in their sheltered nests,
Pluck the down from the ducklings' breasts,
Steal the eggs from the clucking hen,

Ride the pigs round and round the pen!
Here is mischief to spare for all –
Hoity-toity, come at my call!
Tweedledum and Tweedledee,
Come at my summons – come to me!'

Thus said a witch on a windy night,
Then sailed on her broomstick out of sight.

Ruth Bedford

To find out other pranks of witches and goblins read Shakespeare's
A Midsummer Night's Dream, *Act 2, Scene 1, where Puck de-
scribes the fun he has. If you want to know the recipe for a witch's
spell, read Shakespeare's* Macbeth, *Act 4, Scene 1.*

In the next poem, 'The Little Creature', a young child has learnt that her great-grandmother was a witch, and is filled with a fearful foreboding of what may happen when the witches come to claim her as their kin. To really understand the poem you must feel the bewildering shock that the small child is experiencing.

To read the poem effectively, choose seven witches who advance upon the child, pointing bony fingers, each chanting a line in turn and muttering the chorus. The child, in a crescendo of terror, speaks every second line.

The Little Creature

Twinkum, twankum, twirlum and twitch –
My great grandam – She was a Witch.
Mouse in wainscot, Saint in niche –
My great grandam – She was a Witch;
Deadly nightshade flowers in a ditch –
My great grandam – She was a Witch;
Long though the shroud, it grows, stitch by stitch –
My great grandam – She was a Witch;
Wean your weakling before you breech –
My great grandam – She was a Witch;
The fattest pig's but a double flitch –
My great grandam – She was a Witch;
Nightjars rattle, owls scritch –
My great grandam – She was a Witch.

Chorus: Pretty and small,
 A mere nothing at all,
 Pinned up sharp in the ghost of a shawl,
 She'd straddle her down to the kirkyard wall
 And mutter and whisper and call,
 And call . . .

 (Witches vanish)

Child: Red blood out and black blood in,
 My Nannie says I'm a child of sin.
 How did I choose me my witchcraft kin?
 Know I as soon as dark's dreams begin
 Snared is my heart in a nightmare's gin;
 Never from terror I out may win;
 So dawn and dusk I pine, peak, thin,
 Scarcely knowing t'other from which –
 My great grandam – She was a Witch.

Walter de la Mare

33

The next poem hints at the sinister powers of supernatural creatures.
A woman lives alone in a small cottage on a bleak, lonely moor.
One night she hears a pleading voice outside her door . . .

The Witch

Witch: *(in the guise of a young girl, speaking plaintively)*
        I have walked a great while over the snow,
        And I am not tall nor strong.
        My clothes are wet, and my teeth are set,
        And the way was hard and long.
        I have wandered over the fruitful earth,
        But I never came here before.
        Oh, lift me over the threshold, and let me in at
           the door!

Witch: *(knocking at the cottage door)*
        The cutting wind is a cruel foe.
        I dare not stand in the blast.
        My hands are stone, and my voice a groan,
        And the worst of death is past.
        I am but a little maiden still,
        My little white feet are sore
        Oh, lift me over the threshold and let me come
           in at the door!

Woman: *(opens cottage-door and pityingly takes the wretched*
          young girl inside)

Later

Woman: (wild-eyed and shuddering, appears at the door):
      Her voice was the voice that women have
      Who plead for their heart's desire.
      She came – she came – and the quivering flame
      Sank and died in the fire.
      It never was lit again on my hearth
      Since I hurried over the floor,
      To lift her over the threshold and let her in at the
          door.

Mary Coleridge

Study the last stanza carefully.
  What do you think really happened when the witch entered the cottage?
  Think about the deeper meaning of the lines:
    . . . the quivering flame
    Sank and died in the fire.

Overheard on a Saltmarsh

Goblin: Nymph, nymph, what are your beads?
Nymph: Green glass, goblin. Why do you stare at them?
Goblin: Give them me.
Nymph: No.
Goblin: Give them me. Give them me.
Nymph: No.
Goblin: Then I will howl all night in the reeds,
        Lie in the mud and howl for them.
Nymph: Goblin, why do you love them so?
Goblin: They are better than stars or water,
        Better than voices of winds that sing,
        Better than any man's fair daughter,
        Your green glass beads on a silver ring.
Nymph: Hush, I stole them out of the moon.
Goblin: Give me your beads, I want them.
Nymph: No.
Goblin: I will howl in a deep lagoon
        For your green glass beads, I love them so.
        Give them me. Give them.
Nymph: No.

Harold Monro

Acting
To create the atmosphere of the moaning wind, whispering reeds and murmuring water, a group could devise suitable sound effects, and your music teacher might help you to choose some eerie background music. If the lovely nymph's voice is soft and musical, and the greedy goblin's is harsh and throaty, you will give greater impact to the dialogue.

Poetry-Making
Why did the goblin yearn to possess the green glass beads? Add some lines to the dialogue, letting the goblin speak.

Space Travellers

There was a witch, hump-backed and hooded,
Lived by herself in a burnt-out tree;
When storm winds shrieked and the moon was buried
And the dark of the forest was black as black,
She rose in the air like a rocket at sea,
      Riding the wind,
      Riding the night,
Riding the tempest to the moon and back.

There may be a man with a hump of silver,
Telescope eyes and a telephone ear,
Dials to twist and knobs to twiddle,
Waiting for a night when skies are clear,
To shoot from the scaffold with a blazing track,
      Riding the dark,
      Riding the cold,
Riding the silence to the moon and back.

James Nimmo

Why could this poem have been called 'Then and Now'?
Draw or paint two companion pictures illustrating the poem.
Add other selections to this collection of poems about witches. (Robert Herrick, Ben Johnson and Edith Sitwell are some of the other poets who have written on this theme.)
A group might prepare a class radio broadcast entitled 'Do you believe in witches?' You might include information on the traditional haunts of witches; their dress; their 'familiars'; their powers; their spells; any means humans had of combating these spells . . .

Traditionally, humans are supposed to react to ghosts with fear and horror. In the two following poems we encounter frustrated ghosts whose spells do not seem to have worked.

Why is the old wife so unconcerned with the intruders?

How does Colonel Fazackerley turn the tables on the ghost in his house?

Look closely at the last two lines. Is the Colonel really as unconcerned as his heartiness seems to indicate?

The Old Wife and the Ghost

There was an old wife and she lived all alone
    In a cottage not far from Hitchin:
And one bright night, by the full moon light,
    Comes a ghost right into her kitchen.

About that kitchen neat and clean
    The ghost goes pottering round.
But the poor old wife is deaf as a boot
    And so hears never a sound.

The ghost blows up the kitchen fire,
    As bold as bold can be;
He helps himself from the larder shelf,
    But never a sound hears she.

He blows on his hands to make them warm,
    And whistles aloud 'Whee-hee!'
But still as a sack the old soul lies
    And never a sound hears she.

From corner to corner he runs about,
    And into the cupboard he peeps;
He rattles the door and bumps on the floor,
    But still the old wife sleeps.

Jangle and bang go the pots and pans,
    As he throws them all around;
And the plates and mugs and dishes and jugs,
    He flings them all to the ground.

Madly the ghost tears up and down
  And screams like a storm at sea;
And at last the old wife stirs in her bed –
  And it's 'Drat those mice', says she.

Then the first cock crows and morning shows
  And the troublesome ghost's away.
But oh! what a pickle the poor wife sees
  When she gets up next day.

'Them's tidy big mice', the old wife thinks,
  And off she goes to Hitchin,
And a tidy big cat she fetches back
  To keep the mice from her kitchen.

James Reeves

Colonel Fazackerley

Colonel Fazackerley Butterworth-Toast
Bought an old castle complete with a ghost,
But someone or other forgot to declare
To Colonel Fazack that the spectre was there.

On the very first evening, while waiting to dine,
The Colonel was taking a fine sherry wine,
When the ghost, with a furious flash and a flare,
Shot out of the chimney and shivered, 'Beware!'

Colonel Fazackerley put down his glass
And said, 'My dear fellow, that's really first class!
I just can't conceive how you do it at all.
I imagine you're going to a Fancy Dress Ball?'

At this, the dread ghost gave a withering cry.
Said the Colonel (his monocle firm in his eye),
'Now just how you do it I wish I could think.
Do sit down and tell me, and please have a drink.'

The ghost in his phosphorous cloak gave a roar
And floated about between ceiling and floor.
He walked through a wall and returned through a pane
And backed up the chimney and came down again.

Said the Colonel, 'With laughter I'm feeling quite weak!'
(As trickles of merriment ran down his cheek).
'My house-warming party I hope you won't spurn.
You *must* say you'll come and you'll give us a turn!'

At this, the poor spectre – quite out of his wits –
Proceeded to shake himself almost to bits.
He rattled his chains and he clattered his bones
And he filled the whole castle with mumbles and moans.

But Colonel Fazackerley, just as before,
Was simply delighted and called out, 'Encore!'
At which the ghost vanished, his efforts in vain,
And never was seen at the castle again.

'Oh dear, what a pity!' said Colonel Fazack.
'I don't know his name, so I can't call him back.'
And then with a smile that was hard to define,
Colonel Fazackerley went in to dine.

Charles Causley

The last three poems are stories to read and think about. The mysteries of 'The Ballad of Semmerwater' and 'Emperors of the Island' can be explained only if you use your imagination. 'A Strange Meeting' is an experience bordering on the supernatural but with a commonplace explanation. Discuss similar experiences that you yourselves have had.

The Ballad of Semmerwater

Deep asleep, deep asleep,
Deep asleep it lies,
The still lake of Semmerwater
Under the still skies.

And many a fathom, many a fathom,
Many a fathom below,
In a king's tower and a queen's bower
The fishes come and go.

Once there stood by Semmerwater
A mickle town and tall;
King's tower and queen's bower,
And wakeman on the wall.

Came a beggar halt and sore:
'I faint for lack of bread.'
King's tower and queen's bower
Cast him forth unfed.

He knocked at the door of the herdsman's cot,
The herdsman's cot in the dale.
They gave him of their oatcake,
They gave him of their ale.

He has cursed aloud that city proud,
He has cursed it in its pride;
He has cursed it into Semmerwater
Down the brant hillside;
He has cursed it into Semmerwater
There to bide.

King's tower and queen's bower,
And a mickle town and tall;
By glimmer of scale and gleam of fin,
Folk have seen them all.
King's tower and queen's bower,
And weed and reed in the gloom;
And a lost city in Semmerwater,
Deep asleep till Doom.

William Watson

Emperors of the Island

There is the story of a deserted island
where five men walked down to the bay.

The story of this island is
that three men would two men slay.

Three men dug two graves in the sand,
three men stood on the sea wet rock,
three shadows moved away.

There is the story of a deserted island
where three men walked down to the bay.

The story of this island is
that two men would one man slay.

Two men dug one grave in the sand,
two men stood on the sea wet rock,
two shadows moved away.

There is the story of a deserted island
where two men walked down to the bay.

The story of this island is
that one man would one man slay.

One man dug one grave in the sand,
one man stood on the sea wet rock,
one shadow moved away.

There is the story of a deserted island
where four ghosts walked down to the bay.

The story of this island is
that four ghosts would one man slay.

Four ghosts dug one grave in the sand,
four ghosts stood on the sea wet rock;
five ghosts moved away.

Dannie Abse

A Strange Meeting

The moon is full, and so am I;
   The night is late, the ale was good;
And I must go two miles and more
   Along a country road.

Now what is this that's drawing near?
   It seems a man, and tall;
But where the face should show its white
   I see no white at all.

Where is his face: or do I see
   The back part of his head,
And, with his face turned round about,
   He walks this way? I said.

He's close at hand, but where's the face?
   What devil is this I see?
I'm glad my body's warm with ale,
   There's trouble here for me.

I clutch my staff, I make a halt,
   'His blood or mine,' said I.
'Good-night,' the black man said to me,
   As he went passing by.

W. H. Davies

3   Cats and Dogs

Imagine how you would feel if the people you met in the street kept remarking: 'Haven't you got a funny figure!' 'Aren't your legs short and stumpy!' 'Why do you waddle when you walk?' Edward Anthony's dachshund has become very tired of such personal remarks. He would prefer to emphasise his good qualities.

The Dachshund

Because I waddle when I walk,
Should this give rise to silly talk
That I'm ungainly? What's ungainly?
I'm really rather graceful – mainly.
The experts have been known to state
That there's a twinkle in our gait.
One said, 'They have a clumsy grace,'
Which after all is no disgrace.

My funny features may abound:
Short legs, long body, low-to-ground,
But I'm about the perfect pal
For man or woman, boy or gal.
I'm gentle, very playful, kind,
I housebreak fast 'cause I'm refined,
I'm smart but never sly or foxy –
No, do not underrate the dachsie!

Edward Anthony

Write a short poem in which your own dog answers his critics. (Perhaps people have sneered at your bulldog's bandy legs; perhaps someone has laughed at your poodle's latest trim; perhaps the neighbours have accused your alsatian – who can be the gentlest of creatures – of being savage.)

You may like to vary the theme. Your dog, who is admired by everyone, may confide in you that he is really not angelic.

Marguerite Steen, in her book, Little White King, *tells of the doings of Bert, a deaf kitten. Two short passages from the story may give you ideas for making poems of your own.*

Little White King

Now that winter had come, the kitten's afternoons were passed in sleep, unless a brief gleam of sun enticed him out of doors, or the northerly gale, fluttering the dead leaves, tempted him to fling himself about the lawns. He would visit our neighbours, trotting across their grass, lifting his little head, uttering his beguiling *Prr-rr-oo*, and waving his tail in acknowledgment of a caress, before leaping up the pergola, or onto a garage roof, or into the pear tree, where he stood out on a branch, noble as a ship's figurehead, breasting the gale, or, up on the ridge tiles, allowed himself to be blown into a white chrysanthemum by the wind.

Summer loitered imperceptibly into autumn. The sycamores clung to their leaves, then, in two or three sudden gusts, let them down on the lawn. The kitten found a new delight, that of following the gardener as he swung the arc of the broom across and across the grass. Sometimes he became a white windmill, a catherine wheel of silver, cutting indescribable capers among the dry brown flakes that broke into confetti on his back, his flanks and the banner of his tail.

Marguerite Steen

At the Dog Show

(To an Irish Wolfhound)

Long and gray and gaunt he lies,
A Lincoln among dogs; his eyes,
Deep and clear of sight, appraise
The meaningless and shuffling ways
Of human folk that stop to stare.
One witless woman, seeing there
How tired, how contemptuous
He is of all the smell and fuss,
Asks him, 'Poor fellow, are you sick?'

Yea, sick and weary to the quick
Of heat and noise from dawn to dark.
He will not even stoop to bark
His protest, like the lesser bred.

Would he might know, one gazer read
The wistful longing in his face,
The thirst for wind and open space
And stretch of limbs to him begrudged.

There came a little, dapper, fat
And bustling man, with cane and spat
And pearl-gray vest and derby hat –
Such were the judger and the judged!

Christopher Morley

A noble lion lies in a small circus cage. In poetry or prose, describe his feelings and longings.

The monkeys in their cage at the zoo survey the crowds of people watching them. What comments do the monkeys make on human behaviour?

The next three poems are pictures of contentment.

Sunning

Old Dog lay in the summer sun
Much too lazy to rise and run.
He flapped an ear
At a buzzing fly.
He winked a half opened
Sleepy eye.
He scratched himself
On an itching spot,
As he dozed on the porch
Where the sun was hot.
He whimpered a bit
From force of habit
While he lazily dreamed
Of chasing a rabbit.
But Old Dog happily lay in the sun
Much too lazy to rise and run.

James S. Tippett

On a Cat, Ageing

He blinks upon the hearth-rug,
And yawns in deep content,
Accepting all the comforts
That Prov'dence has sent.
Louder he purrs, and louder,
In one glad hymn of praise
For all the night's adventures,
For quiet, restful days.
Life will go on for ever,
With all that cat can wish:
Warmth and the glad procession
Of fish and milk and fish.
Only – the thought disturbs him –
He's noticed once or twice,
The times are somehow breeding
A nimbler race of mice.

Alexander Gray

Inside

A bellyful and the fire,
And him in his old suit,
And me with my heart's desire,
My head across his foot.

And I doze. And he reads.
And the clock ticks slow.
And, though he never heeds,
He knows, and I know.

Presently, without look,
His hand will feel to tug
My ear, his eyes on book,
Mine upon the rug.

Eleanor Farjeon

*The cat and the two dogs in the poems you have just read are warm
and happy, but for different reasons. Explain the reason in each case.*

Read these two short prose descriptions of a dog and a cat 'out for a walk'.

I am fully alive to the pleasure of being invited out for a walk by a dog, who, jumping about and running round me with eloquently wagging tail, looks at me with eyes that plainly say 'Are we going to start?' And when we are fairly off, I like this trusty comrade who sets off at railway speed, remembers that his master cannot follow him at this pace, manifests his pleasure by the friendliest movements, and starts off again, barking an inspiring 'Come on!'

M. Champfleury

When he trots after me and the Black One across rough earth and stones that make his paws sore, something tells him it is not cat behaviour. He will not be carried, because the Black One won't. He dare not stay behind, because if he lost sight of us, he might not find us again. He wants to stop and play with fluttering things in the grass, but he dare not, because he might get lost. If I wait, to pleasure him, he will lapse into gloomy impatience: 'Why don't you go on?' So he keeps trotting at my heels until he is so tired that he drops on his side in a clump of grass. But if I try to pick him up, he leaps away: because that is the way of cat pride.

Marguerite Steen

Watch your own cat or dog when it wants to go out or when it is playing out of doors. After observing carefully, write your description of its behaviour in verse or prose.

It is midnight and the moon is at its full. The house is still for the human beings are fast asleep. But the dog stirs in his kennel, and Minnaloushe, the black cat, prowls through the high grass in the garden.

Dog at Night

At first he stirs uneasily in sleep
And, since the moon does not run off, unfolds
Protesting paws. Grumbling that he must keep
Both eyes awake, he whimpers; then he scolds
And, rising to his feet, demands to know
The stranger's business. You who break the dark
With insolent light, who are you? Where do you go?
But nothing answers his indignant bark.
The moon ignores him, walking on as though
Dogs never were. Stiffened to fury now,
His small hairs stand upright, his howls come fast,
And terrible to hear is the bow-bow
That tears the night. Stirred by this bugle-blast,
The farmer's bitch grows active; without pause
Summons her mastiff and the hound that lies
Three fields away to rally to the cause.
And the next county wakes. And miles beyond
Throats tear themselves and brassy lungs respond
With threats, entreaties, bellowings and cries,
Chasing the white intruder down the skies.

Louis Untermeyer

The Cat and the Moon

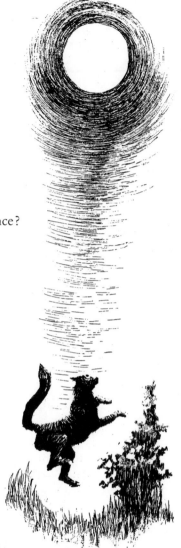

The cat went here and there
And the moon spun round like a top,
And the nearest kin of the moon,
The creeping cat, looked up.
Black Minnaloushe stared at the moon,
For, wander and wail as he would,
The pure cold light in the sky
Troubled his animal blood.
Minnaloushe runs in the grass
Lifting his delicate feet.
Do you dance, Minnaloushe, do you dance?
When two close kindred meet,
What better than call a dance?
Maybe the moon may learn,
Tired of that courtly fashion,
A new dance turn.
Minnaloushe creeps through the grass
From moonlit place to place,
The sacred moon overhead
Has taken a new phase.
Does Minnaloushe know that his pupils
Will pass from change to change,
And that from round to crescent,
From crescent to round they range?
Minnaloushe creeps through the grass
Alone, important and wise,
And lifts to the changing moon
His changing eyes.

W. B. Yeats

Discussion
Both the dog and the cat are stirred by the moon – but they react differ-
ently. How does the dog behave? Find the lines that best show the
sinister link between the moon and the cat.

57

In the two following poems the dog and the cat are restless, and want to be outside – but for different reasons. What is revealed about the character of each creature?

Unsatisfied Yearning

Down in the silent hallway
    Scampers the dog about,
And whines, and barks, and scratches,
    In order to get out.

Once in the glittering starlight,
    He straightway doth begin
To set up a doleful howling
    In order to get in!

Richard Kendall Munkittrick

On a Night of Snow

Cat, if you go outdoors you must walk in the snow,
You will come back with little white shoes on your feet,
Little white slippers of snow that have heels of sleet.
Stay by the fire, my Cat. Lie still, do not go.
See how the flames are leaping and hissing low,
I will bring you a saucer of milk like a marguerite,
So white and so smooth, so spherical and so sweet –
Stay with me, Cat. Outdoors the wild winds blow.

Outdoors the wild winds blow, Mistress, and dark is the
    night,
Strange voices cry in the trees, intoning strange lore,
And more than cats move, lit by our eyes' green light,
On silent feet where the meadow grasses hang hoar –
Mistress, there are portents abroad of magic and might,
And things that are yet to be done. Open the door!

Elizabeth Coatsworth

Have you ever waited and waited for your cat or dog to come home? In that agony of suspense, a host of horrible imaginings disturb you: he may have wandered off and be unable to find his way home; perhaps someone has stolen him; what if he was playing on the road and a car... If you have had such an experience you will be able to sympathise with the writers of the next two poems.

A Child's Dream

-trying to find his dog.

I had a little dog, and my dog was very small;
He licked me in the face, and he answered to my call;
Of all the treasures that were mine, I loved him most of all.

The dog is his treasure

— Simile   His nose was fresh as morning dew and blacker than the
— Rhyme   night; *shiny*
— Personification   I thought that it could even snuff the shadows and the light;
— Alliteration   And his tail he held bravely, like a banner in a fight. *up high*

His body covered thick with hair was very good to smell;
His little stomach underneath was pink as any shell; *quite pink*
And I loved him and honoured him, more than words
    can tell.

We ran out in the morning, both of us, to play,
Up and down across the fields for all the sunny day;
But he ran so swiftly – he ran right away.

to beg seriously

I looked for him, I called for him, entreatingly. Alas,
The dandelions could not speak, though they had seen
    him pass,
And nowhere was his waving tail among the waving grass.

I called him in a thousand ways and yet he did not come;
The pathways and the hedges were horrible and dumb. *stupid*
I prayed to God who never heard. My desperate soul grew
numb. *feel nothing*

The sun sank low. I ran; I prayed: 'If God has not the power
To find him, let me die. I cannot bear another hour.'
When suddenly I came upon a great yellow flower.

And all among its petals, such was Heaven's grace,
In that golden hour, in that golden place, *everything around him was pleasant*
All among its petals, was his hairy face. *① sunset ② he found*

Frances Cornford

The Lost Cat

She took a last and simple meal when there were none to
    see her steal –
    A jug of cream upon the shelf, a fish prepared for dinner;
And now she walks a distant street with delicately sandalled
    feet,
    And no one gives her much to eat or weeps to see her
    thinner.

O my beloved come again, come back in joy, come back
    in pain,
    To end our searching with a mew, or with a purr our
    grieving;
And you shall have for lunch or tea whatever fish swim in
    the sea
    And all the cream that's meant for me – and not a word
    of thieving!

E. V. Rieu

For a Dead Kitten

Put the rubber mouse away,
Pick the spools up from the floor,
What was velvet-shod, and gay,
Will not want them any more.

What was warm, is strangely cold.
Whence dissolved the little breath?
How could this small body hold
So immense a thing as Death?

Sara Henderson Hay

The Death of a Cat

I rose early
On the fourth day
Of his illness,
And went downstairs
To see if he was
All right.
He was not in the
House, and I rushed
Wildly round the
Garden calling his name.
I found him lying
Under a rhododendron
Bush,
His black fur
Wet, and matted
With the dew.
I knelt down beside him,
And he opened his
Mouth as if to
Miaow
But no sound came.
I picked him up
And he lay quietly
In my arms
As I carried him
Indoors.
Suddenly he gave
A quiet miaow
And I felt his body tense
And then lie still.
I had his warm
Lifeless body on
The floor, and
Rubbed my fingers
Through his fur.

A warm tear
Dribbled down
My cheek and
Left a salt taste
On my lips.
I stood up, and
Walked quietly
Out of the room.

Anthony Thompson

63

The next poems probe more deeply into the characters of cats and dogs (although the last one is just as much a character study of men as of cats).

Tim, an Irish Terrier

It's wonderful dogs they're breeding now:
Small as a flea or large as a cow;
But my old lad Tim he'll never be bet
By any dog that he ever met.
'Come on,' says he, 'for I'm not kilt yet.'

No matter the size of the dog he'll meet,
Tim trails his coat the length o' the street,
D'ye mind his scars an' his ragged ear,
The like of a Dublin fusilier?
He's a massacree dog that knows no fear.

But he'd stick to me till his latest breath;
An' he'd go with me to the gates of death.
He'd wait for a thousand years, maybe,
Scratching the door an' whining for me
If I myself were inside in Purgatory.

So I laugh when I hear thim make it plain
That dogs and men never meet again.
For all their talk who'd listen to thim,
With the soul in the shining eyes of him?
Would God be wasting a dog like Tim?

Winifred Letts

Catalogue

Cats sleep fat and walk thin.
Cats, when they sleep, slump;
When they wake, pull in –
And where the plump's been
There's skin.
Cats walk thin.

Cats wait in a lump,
Jump in a streak.
Cats, when they jump, are sleek
As a grape slipping its skin –
They have technique.
Oh, cats don't creak.
They sneak.

Cats sleep fat.
They spread comfort beneath them
Like a good mat,
As if they picked the place
And then sat.
You walk around one
As if he were the City Hall
After that.

If male,
A cat is apt to sing upon a major scale:
This concert is for everybody, this
Is wholesale.
For a baton, he wields a tail.
(He is also found,
When happy, to resound
With an enclosed and private sound.)

A cat condenses.
He pulls in his tail to go under bridges,
And himself to go under fences.
Cats fit
In any size box or kit;
And if a large pumpkin grew under one,
He could arch over it.

When everyone else is just ready to go out,
The cat is just ready to come in.
He's not where he's been.
Cats sleep fat and walk thin.

Rosalie Moore

Men Are Like Cats

MEN
Are like cats.
It's not the smallest use their denying it.
They love sitting beside fires,
Dozing.
They worship food
With an unholy devotion.

They adore comfort,
And yet they will not yield their independence
For these things.
They purr when stroked
The right way;
But they will only be loving
When they feel like it.
And they will not be taught
Tricks.

They are jealous when in love
And also fickle.
They are independent, greedy, selfish,
Athletic when young, lazy, comfort-loving
And yet so charming—
Just like cats.

Mary Carn

The ideas expressed in the poems you have just read are very commonly believed. Traditionally, the dog is regarded as man's loyal friend. In past years a popular name for a pet dog was Fido – the Latin word meaning 'I trust'. You can find a host of stories like Greyfriars Bobby *by E. Atkinson,* That There Dog o' Mine *by Henry Lawson and* Lassie Come Home *by Eric Knight, all of which have this theme. Many people throughout the ages regarded the cat as independent, selfish, arrogant and incapable of loving anyone but itself. (Read Rudyard Kipling's* The Cat that Walked by Himself.*) But these are general ideas, and you should be unwilling to judge any particular cat or dog without making careful studies of it as an individual.*

Karel Capek, in I Had a Dog and a Cat, *made his cat say: 'But you mustn't believe that I care about you. You have warmed me, and now again I shall go and listen to the dark voices.' However, another famous writer, the poet Algernon Charles Swinburne, wrote this tribute to his cat:*

Dogs may fawn on all and some
　　　As they come;
You, a friend of loftier mind,
Answer friends alone in kind.
Just your foot upon my hand
Softly bids it understand.

What kind of a nature has your cat or dog? Write a tribute.

67

4 People

Are you inquisitive about other people? Most of us are. The policeman, of course, is trained to notice details about people so that he can report fully on a person's appearance. But it is much more difficult to get under the skin of another person and really understand his feelings and thoughts. Poets are able to use both kinds of description. Chaucer, a poet of the 14th Century, describes an English housewife of that time. You may find his language strange at first, but when you work it out the appearance of the Wife of Bath will be as clear in your mind as if she were standing in front of you.

The Wife of Bath

Her coverchiefs full finé weren of ground;
I darsté swear they weigheden ten pound
That on a Sunday weren upon her head.
Her hosen weren of fine scarlet red,
Full straight y-tied, and shoes full moist and newé.
Bold was her face, and fair, and red of hué.
She was a worthy woman all her life.

Geoffrey Chaucer

Here is a modern writer's description in prose of Stina, the family cook. Discuss the means by which Chaucer and Herman Smith present the appearance of each woman with startling completeness.

from Stina, The Story of a Cook

I can see her now – small, almost elfin – with the brightest, blackest, wisest eyes I have ever seen. Her face was criss-crossed with innumerable wrinkles which broke into sunbursts when she smiled. . . . In winter she wore a full-gathered skirt of dark-brown wool, a waist buttoned to the brooch of tiny, gold-clasped hands at her throat. A voluminous apron of blue, white-sprigged calico was tied about her waist. Upon her head, which was only slightly gray, she wore a little knitted hood of dark red wool; and often in the morning before the kitchen was warmed up, she wore a sleeveless, knitted woollen vest of the same dark red.

Herman Smith

from Jamaica Inn

He was a great husk of a man, nearly seven feet high, with a creased black brow and a skin the colour of a gypsy. His thick dark hair fell over his eyes in a fringe and hung about his ears. He looked as if he had the strength of a horse, with immense powerful shoulders, long arms that reached almost to his knees, and large fists like hams. His frame was so big that in a sense his head was dwarfed, and sunk between his shoulders, giving that half-stooping impression of a giant gorilla, with his black eyebrows and his mat of hair . . . his nose was hooked, curving to a mouth that might have been perfect once but was now sunken and fallen, and there was still something fine about his great dark eyes, in spite of the lines and pouches and red blood-flecks.

The best things left to him were his teeth, which were all good still, and very white, so that when he smiled they showed up clearly against the tan of his face, giving him the lean and hungry appearance of a wolf.

Daphne du Maurier

Things to do:
In prose or verse, write a description of a class-mate, an entertainer, or some other well-known personality, noting carefully height, weight, build, age, hair, facial features and clothes. Don't mention the name! Let others guess whom you have described.

> Wanted For Murder!

As Sheriff of Dodge City, you have to write a detailed description of the physical appearance of Bronco Bill. Write out the poster that you would circulate to bring about his arrest.

Sometimes poets seize upon special characteristics which they use as clues to character. In the following poems there is no detailed description, but you still get a vivid impression of each person.

Old Dan'l

Out of his cottage to the sun
Bent double comes old Dan'l
His chest all over cotton wool,
His back all over flannel.

'Winter will finish him,' they've said
Each winter now for ten:
But come the first warm day of Spring
Old Dan'l's out again.

L. A. G. Strong

Mrs Button

When Mrs Button, of a morning,
   Comes creaking down the street,
You hear her old two black boots whisper
   'Poor feet—poor feet—poor feet!'

When Mrs Button, every Monday,
   Sweeps the chapel neat,
All down the long, hushed aisles they whisper
   'Poor feet—poor feet—poor feet!'

Mrs Button after dinner
   (It is her Sunday treat)
Sits down and takes her two black boots off
   And rests her two poor feet.

James Reeves

The Shepherd

Old Sam Smith
Lived by himself so long,
He thought three people
A 'turruble throng'.

But he loved 'Old Shep',
Who could open and shut
The hide-hinged door
Of his old bark hut;

And he loved the trees,
The sun and the sky,
And the sound of the wind,
Though he couldn't tell why.

But besides all these,
He loved, to the full,
The smell of the sheep,
And the greasy wool.

So they buried him out
(For at last he died)
Out, all alone,
On a bleak hill side,

And there's never a sound
But the bleat of the sheep,
As they nibble the mound
That marks his sleep.

Mary Gilmore

The Sweet-Tooth

Taking a turn after tea
Through orchards of Mirabellea,
Where clusters of yellow and red
Dangled and glowed overhead,
Who should I see
But old Timothy,
Hale and hearty as hearty can be—
Timothy under the crab-apple tree.

His blue eyes twinkling at me,
Munching and crunching with glee,
And wagging his wicked old head,
'I've still got a sweet-tooth', he said—
A hundred and three
Come January,
I've one tooth left in my head, said he,
Timothy under the crab-apple tree.

Wilfrid Gibson

You will now read of two everyday people – a schoolboy and a teacher.
Read the poems carefully to see how the poets describe not only personal
appearance but probe into their subjects' problems.

Timothy Winters

Timothy Winters comes to school
With eyes as wide as a football-pool,
Ears like bombs and teeth like splinters:
A blitz of a boy is Timothy Winters.

His belly is white, his neck is dark,
And his hair is an exclamation-mark.
His clothes are enough to scare a crow
And through his britches the blue winds blow.

When teacher talks he won't hear a word
And he shoots down dead the arithmetic-bird,
He licks the patterns off his plate
And he's not even heard of the Welfare State.

Timothy Winters has bloody feet
And he lives in a house on Suez Street,
He sleeps in a sack on the kitchen floor
And they say there aren't boys like him any more.

Old Man Winters likes his beer
And his missus ran off with a bombardier,
Grandma sits in the grate with a gin
And Timothy's dosed with an aspirin.

The Welfare Worker lies awake
But the law's as tricky as a ten-foot snake,
So Timothy Winters drinks his cup
And slowly goes on growing up.

At Morning Prayers the Headmaster helves
For children less fortunate than ourselves,
And the loudest response in the room is when
Timothy Winters roars 'Amen!'

So come one angel, come on ten:
Timothy Winters says 'Amen
Amen amen amen amen.'
Timothy Winters, Lord.
                Amen.

Charles Causley

Schoolmaster

The window gives onto the white trees.
The master looks out of it at the trees,
for a long time, he looks for a long time
out through the window at the trees,
breaking his chalk slowly in one hand.
And it's only the rules of long division.
And he's forgotten the rules of long division.
Imagine not remembering long division!
A mistake on the blackboard, a mistake.

We watch him with a different attention
needing no one to hint to us about it,
there's more than difference in this attention.
The schoolmaster's wife has gone away,
we do not know where she has gone to,
we do not know why she has gone,
what we know is his wife has gone away.

His clothes are neither new nor in the fashion;
wearing the suit which he always wears
and which is neither new nor in the fashion
the master goes downstairs to the cloakroom.
He fumbles in his pocket for a ticket.
'What's the matter? Where is that ticket?
Perhaps I never picked up my ticket.
Where is the thing?' Rubbing his forehead.
'Oh, here it is. I'm getting old.
Don't argue auntie dear, I'm getting old.
You can't do much about getting old.'
We hear the door below creaking behind him.

The window gives onto the white trees.
The trees there are high and wonderful,
but they are not why we are looking out.
We look in silence at the schoolmaster.

He has a bent back and clumsy walk,
he moves without defences, clumsily,
worn out I ought to have said, clumsily.
Snow falling on him softly through the silence
turns him to white under the white trees.
A little longer will make him so white
we shall not see him in the whitened trees.

Yevgeny Yevtushenko
(translated by Robin Milner-Gulland
and Peter Levi, S. J.)

Poetry isn't a camera, giving us just what is seen. The poet sees in a different way, and, being a shrewd judge of people he often lets his characters reveal themselves by their own remarks, as do the people in the next poems.

The Wife's Lament

My life is like daytime
With no sun to warm it!
My life is like night
With no glimmer of moon!
And I—the young woman—
Am like the swift steed
On the curb, the young swallow
With wings crushed and broken;
My jealous old husband
Is drunken and snoring,
But even while snoring,
He keeps one eye open,
And watches me always,
Me, poor little wife!

(Written by the Russian Nikolay Nekrasov, and translated by Juliet M. Soskice.)

The Housewife's Lament

One day I was walking, I heard a complaining
And saw an old woman the picture of gloom.
She gazed at the mud on her doorstep, 'twas raining,
And this was her song as she wielded her broom.

O life is a toil, and love is a trouble.
Beauty will fade and riches will flee.
Pleasures they dwindle and prices they double
And nothing is as I would wish it to be.

There's too much of worriment goes to a bonnet,
There's too much of ironing goes to a shirt,
There's nothing that pays for the time that you waste
    on it,
There's nothing that lasts but trouble and dirt.

In March it is mud, it is slush in December,
The mid-summer breezes are loaded with dust.
In fall the leaves litter, in muddy September
The wallpaper rots and the candlesticks rust.

It's sweeping at six and it's dusting at seven.
It's victuals at eight and it's dishes at nine.
It's potting and panning from ten to eleven.
We've scarce finished breakfast, we're ready to dine.

Last night in my dreams I was stationed forever
On a far little rock in the midst of the sea.
My one chance of life was a ceaseless endeavour
To sweep off the waves as they swept over me.

Alas! 'Twas no dream; ahead I behold it,
I see I am helpless my fate to avert.
She lay down her broom, her apron she folded,
She lay down and died, and was buried in dirt.

Anon.

Miss Wing

At the end of the street lives small Miss Wing,
A feathery, fluttery bird of a thing.
If you climb the street to the very top,
There you will see her fancy shop
With ribbons and buttons and frills and fluffs,
Pins and needles, purses and puffs,

Cosies and cushions and bits of chiffon,
And tiny hankies for ladies to sniff on,
And twists of silk and pieces of lace,
And odds and ends all over the place.
You push the door and the door-bell rings,
And the voice you hear is little Miss Wing's.
'Good-day, my dear, and how do you do?
Now tell me, what can I do for you?
Just half a second, please, dear Miss Gay –
As I was saying the other day –
Now what did I do with that so-and-so?
I'm sure I had it a moment ago –
As I was saying – why, yes, my dear –
A very nice day for the time of the year –
Have you heard how poor Mrs Such-and-such? –
Oh, I hope I haven't charged too much;
That would never do – Now, what about pink?
It's nice for children, I always think –
Some buttons to go with a lavender frock?
Why now, I believe I'm out of stock –
Well, what about these? Oh, I never knew –
I'm ever so sorry – now what about blue?
Such a very nice woman – a flower for a hat?'
And so she goes on, with 'Fancy that!'
And 'You never can tell,' and 'Oh dear, no,'
And 'There now! it only goes to show.'

And on she goes like a hank of tape,
A reel of ribbon, a roll of crêpe,
Till you think her tongue will never stop.
And that's Miss Wing of the fancy shop.

James Reeves

*From reading 'Sir Smasham Uppe', what do you learn of the characters
of Sir Smasham and his host?*

Sir Smasham Uppe

Good afternoon, Sir Smasham Uppe!
We're having tea: do take a cup!
Sugar and milk? Now let me see –
Two lumps, I think? . . . Good gracious me!
The silly thing slipped off your knee!
Pray don't apologise, old chap:
A very trivial mishap!
So clumsy of you? How absurd!
My dear Sir Smasham, not a word!
Now do sit down and have another,
And tell us all about your brother –
You know, the one who broke his head.
Is the poor fellow still in bed?
A chair – allow me, sir! . . . Great Scott!
That *was* a nasty smash! Eh, what?
Oh, not at all: the chair was old –
Queen Anne, or so we have been told.
We've got at least a dozen more:
Just leave the pieces on the floor.
I want you to admire our view:
Come nearer to the window, do;
And look how beautiful . . . Tut, tut!
You didn't see that it was shut?
I hope you are not badly cut!

Not hurt? A fortunate escape!
Amazing! Not a single scrape!
And now, if you have finished tea,
I fancy you might like to see
A little thing or two I've got.
That china plate? Yes, worth a lot:
A beauty too ... Ah, there it goes!
I trust it didn't hurt your toes?
Your elbow brushed it off the shelf?
Of course: I've done the same myself.
And now, my dear Sir Smasham – oh,
You surely don't intend to go?
You *must* be off? Well, come again.
So glad you're fond of porcelain!

E. V. Rieu

One of the characteristics of old age is the tendency to live in the past. Notice how the poet uses pictures, sounds and even his verse-form to interweave the reality of Mrs Dixon's present life with her memories of the past.

Once at Wiseman's Ferry

Mrs Dixon had ducks,
    Shamefully greedy young sinners,
But duck by duck –
It was very hard luck –
    All those dillies were dinners.
For the week-end travellers came by car,
From north and south, and from near and far;
Said Mrs Dixon, 'My roast ducks are
    Wonderful money spinners.'

Now Mrs Dixon is old, and still
She lives in the cottage below the hill,
The river runs silver beside her door,
The she-oaks feather the darkening shore;

She sits and sinks in her cushioned chair,
Pillows her head of silvery hair,
And dozes and dreams about days of yore.

Up on the hill,
    Last night is falling,
    Wild birds are calling,

Sweet and shrill,
    Bell-clear and keen,
    All unseen,

Babble and trill.
Deereeree chatters and currawongs scold,
'Come along, come along,' hasty and bold;
Thrushes are whistling, coachwhips crack,
Magpies warble, then, '*Quack, quack, quack*' –
All Mrs Dixon's ducks are back.

She rubs her eyes and she leaves her chair,
Looks on the yard – no ducks are there.
No dillies paddle beside the shore,
All of them gone ten years or more;
Only their voices haunt the air,
Only their gabble, mocking her still,
Out of the shadows up on the hill.

Then all the voices, as one voice, cease.
    Arms of darkness enfold the brush,
    Deereeree, currawong, magpie, thrush,
All at peace.
In a hush profound,
A lyre-bird steps from his dancing mound.

Ella McFadyen

83

5 Reading Aloud

People at work and at play enjoy singing together. Workmen pulling heavily laden barges sang 'The Volga Boatmen'; negro slaves heaving huge bales of cotton sang 'Ol' Man River'; and sailors hauling in ropes and anchor-chains sang 'Blow the Man Down'. Their singing together helped them keep regular rhythms in their movements.

Now this is the first rule for reading poetry aloud in groups – you must keep together! Of course, if you chant monotonously, the result will be too mechanical. Hence, the second rule – your voices must convey not only the rhythm, *but also the* meaning of what you are reading. *Lilting lines need high, light voices – girls do well here; pounding lines need low, heavy voices – boys help here.*

We have made suggestions for solo and group voices in some cases; but, of course, you may vary our 'arrangements' to suit your own class.

Hunting Song

The fox he came lolloping, lolloping,
Lolloping. His eyes were bright,
His ears were high.
He was like death at the end of a string
When he came to the hollow
Log. He ran in one side
And out of the other. O
He was sly.

The hounds they came tumbling, tumbling,
Tumbling. Their heads were low,
Their eyes were red.
The sound of their breath was louder than death
When they came to the hollow
Log. They boiled at one end
But a bitch found the scent. O
They were mad.

The hunter came galloping, galloping,
Galloping. All damp was his mare
From her hooves to her mane.
His coat and his mouth were redder than death
When he came to the hollow
Log. He took in the rein
And over he went. O
He was fine.

The log he just lay there, alone in
The clearing. No fox nor hound
Nor mounted man
Saw his black round eyes in their perfect disguise
(As the ends of a hollow
Log). He watched death go through him,
Around him and over him. O
He was wise.

Donald Finkel

The following poem provides opportunities for miming the instruments. Organise your group so that each musical instrument is represented by a group member, and the other parts are read by the class in chorus. A conductor may be useful to help you vary the rate of speaking for special effects, and to ensure an increasing crescendo of sound.

The Ceremonial Band

The old King of Dorchester,
He had a little orchestra,
And never did you hear such a ceremonial band.
'Tootle-too,' said the flute,
'Deed-a-reedle,' said the fiddle,
For the fiddles and the flutes were the finest in the land.

The old King of Dorchester,
He had a little orchestra,
And never did you hear such a ceremonial band.
'Pump-a-rum,' said the drum,
'Tootle-too,' said the flute,
'Deed-a-reedle,' said the fiddle,
For the fiddles and the flutes were the finest in the land.

The old King of Dorchester,
He had a little orchestra,
And never did you hear such a ceremonial band.
'Pickle-pee,' said the fife,
'Pump-a-rum,' said the drum,
'Tootle-too,' said the flute,
'Deed-a-reedle,' said the fiddle,
For the fiddles and the flutes were the finest in the land.

The old King of Dorchester,
He had a little orchestra,
And never did you hear such a ceremonial band.
'Zoomba-zoom,' said the bass,
'Pickle-pee,' said the fife,
'Pump-a-rum,' said the drum,
'Tootle-too,' said the flute,
'Deed-a-reedle,' said the fiddle,
For the fiddles and the flutes were the finest in the land.

The old King of Dorchester,
He had a little orchestra,
And never did you hear such a ceremonial band.
'Pah-pa-rah,' said the trumpet,
'Zoomba-zoom,' said the bass,
'Pickle-pee,' said the fife,
'Pump-a-rum,' said the drum,
'Tootle-too,' said the flute,
'Deed-a-reedle,' said the fiddle,
For the fiddles and the flutes were the finest in the land,
Oh! the fiddles and the flutes were the finest in the land!

James Reeves

Wilfrid Noyce was one of the British expedition that succeeded in climbing Mount Everest. In his account of this feat, South Col, *Noyce describes his climb. 'A dead weight, two long leaden arms, began dragging at my two shoulders. Curious things were beginning to happen to my breath, to my mind. As in a dream I was back at the end of the cross-country course at Charterhouse. I was spattered with mud, breathing hoarsely, exhausted. Now somebody was asking me to run the thing again. No, it was too much.'*

    Read his account in verse – 'Breathless'.

    Consider: why he has written in this form – very short lines, but one very long stanza;

              why he uses such short words and jerky phrases;

              why he repeats the same words and phrases.

Which account (prose or poetry) makes a greater impression on you? Now, read the poem aloud.

Breathless

Heart aches,
Lungs pant
The dry air
Sorry, scant.
Legs lift
And why at all?
Loose drift,
Heavy fall.
Prod the snow
Is easiest way;
A flat step
Is holiday.
Look up,
The far stone
Is many miles
Far and alone.
Grind the breath
Once more and on;
Don't look up
Till journey's done
Must look up,

Glasses are dim.
Wrench of hand
Is breathless limb.
Pause one step,
Breath swings back;
Swallow once,
Dry throat is slack,
Then on
To the far stone;
Don't look up,
Counts the steps done.
One step,
One heart-beat,
Stone no nearer
Dragging feet.
Heart aches,
Lungs pant
The dry air
Sorry, scant.

Wilfrid Noyce

Arrange the following poems yourselves, for group-speaking with solo voices and chorus.

Keep the movement of the lines clear and definite.

Beware of 'tongue-twisting' the sounds.

Remember that a crescendo of sound can be created by adding voices, and a diminution by subtracting voices. Both of these poems offer you chances to experiment with this sort of pattern in sound.

The End of the Road

In these boots, and with this staff
Two hundred leaguers and a half –
Two hundred leaguers and a half –
Walked I, went I, paced I, tripped I,
Marched I, held I, skelped I, slipped I,
Pushed I, panted, swung and dashed I;
Picked I, forded, swam and splashed I,
Strolled I, climbed I, crawled and scrambled,
Dropped and dipped I, ranged and rambled;
Plodded I, hobbled I, trudged and tramped I,
And in lonely spinnies camped I,
And in haunted pinewoods slept I.
Lingered, loitered, limped and crept I,
Clambered, halted, stepped and leapt I;
Slowly sauntered, roundly strode I,
And. . . .
Let me not conceal it. . . . Rode I.

(For who but critics could complain
of 'riding' in a railway train?)

Across the valleys and the high-land,
With all the world on either hand,
Drinking when I had a mind to,
Singing when I felt inclined to;
Nor ever turned my face to home
Till I had slaked my heart at Rome.

Hilaire Belloc

The Storm

First there were two of us, then there were three of us,
Then there was one bird more,
Four of us – wild white sea-birds,
Treading the ocean floor;
And the *wind* rose, and the *sea* rose,
To the angry billows' roar –
With one of us – two of us – three of us – four of us
Sea-birds on the shore.

Soon there were five of us, soon there were nine of us,
And lo! in a trice sixteen!
And the yeasty surf curdled over the sands,
The gaunt grey rocks between;
And the tempest raved, and the lightning's fire
Struck blue on the spindrift hoar –
And on four of us – ay, and on four times four of us
Sea-birds on the shore.

And our sixteen waxed to thirty-two,
And they past three score –
A wild, white welter of winnowing wings,
And ever more and more;
And the winds lulled, and the sea went down,
And the sun streamed out on high,
Gilding the pools and the spume and the spars
'Neath the vast blue deeps of the sky;
And the isles and the bright green headlands shone,
As they'd never shone before,
Mountains and valleys of silver cloud,
Wherein to swing, sweep, soar –
A host of screeching, scolding, scrabbling
Sea-birds on the shore –
A snowy, silent, sun-washed drift
Of sea-birds on the shore.

Walter de la Mare

Annabel Lee

It was many and many a year ago,
    In a kingdom by the sea,
That a maiden there lived whom you may know
    By the name of Annabel Lee;
And this maiden she lived with no other thought
    Than to love and be loved by me.

I was a child and she was a child,
    In this kingdom by the sea;
But we loved with a love that was more than love –
    I and my Annabel Lee;
With a love that the wingèd seraphs of heaven
    Coveted her and me.

And this was the reason that, long ago,
    In this kingdom by the sea,
A wind blew out of a cloud, chilling
    My beautiful Annabel Lee;
So that her high born kinsmen came
    And bore her away from me,
To shut her up in a sepulchre
    In this kingdom by the sea.

The angels, not half so happy in heaven,
    Went envying her and me –
Yes! – that was the reason (as all men know,
    In this kingdom by the sea)
That the wind came out of the cloud by night,
    Chilling and killing my Annabel Lee.

But our love it was stronger by far than the love
  Of those who were older than we –
  Of many far wiser than we –
And neither the angels in heaven above,
  Nor the demons down under the sea,
Can ever dissever my soul from the soul
  Of the beautiful Annabel Lee.

For the moon never beams without bringing me dreams
  Of the beautiful Annabel Lee;
And the stars never rise but I feel the bright eyes
  Of the beautiful Annabel Lee;
And so, all the night-tide, I lie down by the side
Of my darling – my darling – my life and my bride,
  In the sepulchre there by the sea,
  In her tomb by the sounding sea.

Edgar Allan Poe

'Cows' *is a poem for reading at a leisurely pace. The solo speakers,*
brown cow and white cow, are certainly laconic, but there is a clever
differentiation in character. The tone of your voices should change to
indicate this.

Cows

Half the time they munched the grass, and all the time they
    lay
Down in the water-meadows, the lazy month of May,
         A-chewing,
         A-mooing,
      To pass the hours away.
      'Nice weather,' said the brown cow.
        'Ah,' said the white.
      'Grass is very tasty.'
        'Grass is all right.'

Half the time they munched the grass, and all the time they
    lay
Down in the water-meadows, the lazy month of May,
            A-chewing,
            A-mooing,
       To pass the hours away.
     'Rain coming,' said the brown cow.
       'Ah,' said the white.
     'Flies is very tiresome.'
       'Flies bite.'

Half the time they munched the grass, and all the time they
    lay
Down in the water-meadows, the lazy month of May,
            A-chewing,
            A-mooing,
       To pass the hours away.
     'Time to go,' said the brown cow.
       'Ah,' said the white.
     'Nice chat.' 'Very pleasant.'
       'Night.' 'Night.'

Half the time they munched the grass, and all the time they
    lay
Down in the water-meadows, the lazy month of May,
            A-chewing,
            A-mooing,
       To pass the hours away.

James Reeves

Ballads lend themselves to expressive reading aloud because they have regular rhythms and tell stories. Moreover, because they have plenty of direct action expressed in dialogue, ballads are very suitable for acting.

It is obvious that 'Soldier, Soldier' is a dialogue, but you will need six readers for 'The Maid Freed from the Gallows', as the poem falls into a distinct pattern – the maid pleads with the judge, then with her father, her mother, her brother, her sister and her true-love in turn, and each replies to her. 'Young Waters' has been arranged as a reading; in a similar way arrange 'The Twa Brothers'.

Soldier, Soldier

Soldier, soldier, won't you marry me?
With your musket, fife and drum.
How can I marry such a pretty girl as you
When I've got no hat to put on?

Off to the tailor she did go
As hard as she could run,
Brought him back the finest that was there.
Now, soldier, put it on.

Soldier, soldier, won't you marry me?
With your musket, fife and drum.
How can I marry such a pretty girl as you
When I've got no coat to put on?

Off to the tailor she did go
As hard as she could run,
Brought him back the finest that was there.
Now, soldier, put it on.

Soldier, soldier, won't you marry me?
With your musket, fife and drum.
How can I marry such a pretty girl as you
When I've got no shoes to put on?

Off to the shoe shop she did go
As hard as she could run,
Brought him back the finest that was there.
Now, soldier, put them on.

Soldier, soldier, won't you marry me?
With your musket, fife and drum.
How can I marry such a pretty girl as you
With a wife and baby at home?

Anon.

The Maid Freed From the Gallows

'O good Lord Judge, and sweet Lord Judge,
    Peace for a little while!
Methinks I see my own father,
    Come riding by the stile.

'Oh father, oh father, a little of your gold,
    And likewise of your fee!
To keep my body from yonder grave,
    And my neck from the gallows-tree.'

'None of my gold now you shall have,
    Nor likewise of my fee;
For I am come to see you hangd,
    And hangèd you shall be.'

'Oh good Lord Judge, and sweet Lord Judge,
    Peace for a little while!
Methinks I see my own mother,
    Come riding by the stile.

'Oh mother, oh mother, a little of your gold,
    And likewise of your fee,
To keep my body from yonder grave,
    And my neck from the gallows-tree!'

'Oh good Lord Judge, and sweet Lord Judge,
    Peace for a little while!
Methinks I see my own brother,
    Come riding by the stile.

'Oh brother, oh brother, a little of your gold,
    And likewise of your fee,
To keep my body from yonder grave,
    And my neck from the gallows-tree!'

'None of my gold now shall you have,
    Nor likewise of my fee;
For I am come to see you hangd,
    And hangèd you shall be.'

'None of my gold now shall you have,
    Nor likewise of my fee;
For I am come to see you hangd,
    And hangèd you shall be.'

'Oh good Lord Judge, and sweet Lord Judge,
    Peace for a little while!
Methinks I see my own sister,
    Come riding by the stile.

'Oh sister, oh sister, a little of your gold,
    And likewise of your fee,
To keep my body from yonder grave,
    And my neck from the gallows-tree!'

'None of my gold now shall you have,
    Nor likewise of my fee;
For I am come to see you hangd,
    And hangèd you shall be.'

'Oh good Lord Judge, and sweet Lord Judge,
    Peace for a little while!
Methinks I see my own true-love,
    Come riding by the stile.

'Oh true-love, oh true-love, a little of your gold,
    And likewise of your fee,
To save my body from yonder grave,
    And my neck from the gallows-tree.'

'Some of my gold now you shall have,
    And likewise of my fee,
For I am come to see you saved,
    And savèd you shall be.'

Anon.

Young Waters

Narrator:

About Yule, when the wind blew cule,
    And the round tables began,
A there is cum to our king's court
    Mony a well-favourd man.

The queen luikt owre the castle-wa,
    Beheld baith dale and down,
And then she saw Young Waters
    Cum riding to the town.

His footmen they did rin before,
    His horsemen rade behind;
Ane mantel of the burning gowd
    Did keip him frae the wind.

Gowden-graithd his horse before,
    And siller-shod behind;
The horse Young Waters rade upon
    Was fleeter than the wind.

Out then spake a wylie lord,
    Unto the queen said he,

Lord:

'O tell me wha's the fairest face
    Rides in the company?'

Queen: 'I've sene lord, and I've sene laird,
                And knights of high degree,
            But a fairer face than Young Waters
                Mine eyne did never see.'

Narrator: Out then spack the jealous king,
                And an angry man was he:
King: 'O if he had bin twice as fair,
                You micht have excepted me.'

Queen: 'You're neither laird nor lord,' she says,
                'Bot the king that wears the crown;
            There is not a knight in fair Scotland
                But to thee maun bow down.'

Narrator: For a' that she could do or say,
                Appeas'd he wad nae bee,
            Bot for the words which she had said,
                Young Waters he maun die.

            They hae taen Young Waters,
                And put fetters to his feet;
            They hae taen Young Waters,
                And thrown him in dungeon deep.

Young Waters: 'Aft I have ridden thro Stirling town
                In the wind bot and the weit;
            Bot I neir rade thro Stirling town
                Wi fetters at my feet.

            'Aft I have ridden thro Stirling town
                In the wind bot and the rain;
            Bot I neir rade thro Stirling town
                Neir to return again.'

Narrator: They hae taen to the heiding-hill
              His young son in his craddle,
         And they hae taen to the heiding-hill
              His horse bot and his saddle.

They hae taen to the heiding-hill
     His lady fair to see,
And for the words the queen had spoke
     Young Waters he did die.

Anon.

The Twa Brothers

There were twa brethren in the North,
  They went to school thegither;
The one unto the other said,
  'Will you try a warsle, brither?'

They warsled up, they warsled down,
  Till Sir John fell to the ground,
And there was a knife in Sir Willie's pouch
  Gied him a deadly wound.

'Tak' aff, tak' aff my holland sark,
  Rive it frae gare to gare,
And stap it in my bleeding wound –
  'Twill aiblins bleed nae mair.'

He's puit aff his holland sark,
  Rave it frae gare to gare,
And stapt it in his bleeding wound –
  But aye it bled the mair.

'O tak' now aff my green cleiding
  And row me saftly in.
And carry me up to Chester kirk,
  Whar the grass grows fair and green.

'But what will ye say to your father dear
  When ye gae home at e'en?' –
'I'll say ye're lying at Chester kirk,
  Whar the grass grows fair and green.' –

'O no, O no, when he speers for me
  Saying, 'William, whar is John?'
Ye'll say ye left me at Chester school
  Leaving the school alone.'

He's ta'en him up upo' his back,
   And borne him hence away,
And carried him to Chester kirk,
   And laid him in the clay.

But when he sat in his father's chair,
   He grew baith pale and wan:
'O what blude's that upon your brow?
   And whar is your brither John?'

'O John's awa' to Chester school,
   A scholar he'll return;
He bade me tell his father dear
   About him no' to mourn.

'And it is the blude 'o my gude grey steed;
   He wadna hunt for me.' —
'O thy steed's blude was ne'er so red,
   Nor ne'er so dear to me!

'And whaten blude's that upon your dirk?
   Dear Willie, tell to me.' —
'It is the blude o' my ae brither
   And dule and wae is me!' —

'O what sall I say to your mither?
   Dear Willie, tell to me.' —
'I'll saddle my steed and awa' I'll ride,
   To dwell in some far countrie.' —

'O when will ye come hame again?
   Dear Willie, tell to me!' —
'When the sun and moon dance on yon green:
   And that will never be!'

                              Anon.

---

warsle – wrestle, gare – gore, row – wrap, rive – tear, aiblins – perhaps,
cleiding – clothing, speers – asks.

Things to do

Re-read the ballads and find evidence in them that the following state-ments are true:
   Many ancient ballads are written down in dialect.
   There is much repetition *in ballad poetry.*
   Ballad themes are grim and blood-thirsty.
   A ballad plunges into the story, for it is the story *that is important.*
   The minstrel often used a refrain *in his ballad.*
   Ballads have a distinct rhythm.
   There is much dialogue *in ballads.*
   Ballads always have rhyme.

Remembering the essential qualities of ballad-poetry, try writing your own ballads.
   Perhaps these themes may help you:
   '*Sir Eglamore was a valiant knight who went to fight a dragon. From morn to eve the fight lasted; but the dragon's hide was so tough that Sir Eglamore's sword could not penetrate it. However, the dragon grew weary as night fell, and he gave a mighty yawn. Into that gaping throat, Sir Eglamore thrust his brave blade, hilt and all! For this courageous deed (of course the King didn't know the truth) Sir Eglamore was rewarded with the hand of the Princess.'*
   '*Lady Margaret, lovely and fair, loved the gallant and brave Sir Hugh. Their marriage was forbidden by Margaret's father. So the pair were secretly wed and fled away together. Out rode her father in mur-derous rage and pursued the lovers to the ocean's cliffs. There he slew Sir Hugh, and, at this, Lady Margaret flung herself over the cliffs. 'Tis said that on stormy evenings, when the moon's a crescent in the sky, the lovers walk along those cliffs.'*

6 Fun and Nonsense

You have probably realised, ever since you heard your first nursery
rhymes, that there is a fascination in strange words, lively rhythm and
a pattern of sounds – even if the words don't make sense.

One of the two 'nonsense' rhymes that follow is a traditional York-
shire jingle, and the record is a similar one from the south of England.

As I went up the humber jumber,
Humberjumberjeenio,
There I met Sir Hoker Poker
Carrying away campeenio.
If I'd had my tit-for-tat,
My tit-for-tat, myteenio,
I'd never have let Sir Hoker Poker
Carry away campeenio.

As I went up my umligumli,
Umligumligeeni,
There I saw Sir Ackamajack
Eating my alicofeeni,
Oh! If I had my ansicansi,
Ansicansiceeni,
Wouldn't I give it Sir Ackamajack
For eating my alicofeeni.

See how quickly you can learn these jingles off by heart. Have a guess
at their meanings. (They are slightly different.) The translation is
given at the end of the chapter, but don't look until you have written
your own version and compared it with the efforts of other class members.

Many nonsense poems have been written about animals.

The Lion and the Tiger

The Lion, the Lion, he dwells in the waste,
He has a big head and a very small waist;
But his shoulders are stark, and his jaws they are grim,
And a good little child will not play with him.

The Tiger, on the other hand, is kittenish and mild,
He makes a pretty playfellow for any little child;
And mothers of large families (who claim to common-
    sense)
Will find a Tiger will repay the trouble and expense.

Hilaire Belloc

The Rhinoceros

The rhino is a homely beast,
For human eyes he's not a feast.
But you and I will never know
Why nature chose to make him so.
Farewell, farewell, you old rhinoceros,
I'll stare at something less prepoceros!

Ogden Nash

If You Should Meet a Crocodile

— Rhyme
— Personification

If you should meet a crocodile,
  Don't take a stick and poke him;
Ignore the welcome in his smile,
  Be careful not to stroke him.
For as he sleeps upon the Nile,
  He thinner gets and thinner;
And whene'er you meet a crocodile
  He's ready for his dinner.

Anon.

Anonymous

You might like to learn this group of poems, too. When you have mastered their rhythms, try writing other 'odd animal' tales in verse. For example, you might begin:

'If you should meet a kangaroo . . .'
'The camel, the camel, it lives . . .'
'The wombat has a low I.Q. . . .'

Limericks

An epicure dining at Crewe,
Once found a large mouse in his stew.
   Said the waiter, 'Don't shout
   And wave it about,
Or the rest will be wanting one, too.'

A sea-serpent saw a big tanker,
Bit a hole in her side and then sank her.
   It swallowed the crew
   In a minute or two,
And then picked its teeth with the anchor.

There was a young lady of Ryde;
Of eating green apples she died.
   Inside the lamented
   The apples fermented
And made cider inside her inside.

A cheerful old bear at the zoo
Could always find something to do.
   When it bored him you know,
   To walk to and fro,
He reversed – and he walked fro and to.

Before attempting to write similar verses, study the limerick pattern. The first, second and fifth lines must rhyme, and each must have three strong beats; the third and fourth lines must rhyme, and each must have two strong beats. Try to finish your verse with a 'sting in the tail' – an unexpected or funny last line. As subjects for your limericks you could use the names of your own suburbs or towns.

The Vet

To be a successful and competent vet,
   Needs knowledge exceedingly wide,
For each of the patients he's likely to get
   Possesses a different inside.

He must know why the cat is refusing her milk,
   Why the dog is not eating his bone,
Why the coat of the horse is not shining like silk,
   Why the parrot does nothing but groan;

Why the ducks and the chickens are failing to lay,
   Why so faint the canary bird sings,
And if he is called to the Zoo he must say
   An incredible number of things.

    If the lion's caught a cold,
    If the zebra's getting old,
If the centipede has trouble with his feet,
    If the hippo's feeling ill,
    If the bison's got a chill,
If the Arctic fox is suffering from heat,

    If some virulent disease
    Has attacked the chimpanzees,
If the tortoise hasn't stirred for several years,
    If the bear's too full of buns,
    If the cobra eats her sons,
If the panther has a wife who chews his ears;

    If giraffes have had a tiff
    And their necks are feeling stiff,
If hyenas will not laugh at keepers' jokes,
    If the monkey's pinched his tail,
    If the rhino's looking pale,
If the elephant eats paper-bags and chokes,

If the camel hurts his hump,
If the kangaroo won't jump,
If the crocodile turns cannibal and bites,
They run away and get
That omniscient, the vet
And expect him to put everything to rights.

Profoundly I pity the vet, who must learn
Such a very great deal for his pay;
My son, I advise you most strongly to earn
Your living an easier way.

Don't attempt to attend the zoological crowd;
A far more advisable plan,
Is to call yourself 'Doctor', and so be allowed
To specialise only on Man.

Guy Boas

The Fisherman

Upon the river's bank serene
A fisher sat where all was green,
   And looked it.

He saw when light was growing dim
The fish, or else the fish saw him,
   And hooked it.

He took with high erected comb
The fish, or else the story, home,
   And cooked it.

Recording angels by his bed
Weighed all that he had done or said –
   And booked it!

Four Authors

The Microscope

Anton Leeuwenhoek was Dutch.
He sold pincushions, cloth, and such.
The waiting townsfolk fumed and fussed
As Anton's dry goods gathered dust.

He worked, instead of tending store,
At grinding special lenses for
A microscope. Some of the things
He looked at were:
                                    mosquitoes' wings,
the hairs of sheep, the legs of lice,
the skin of people, dogs, and mice;
ox eyes, spiders' spinning gear,
fishes' scales, a little smear
of his own blood,
                                    and best of all,
the unknown, busy, very small
bugs that swim and bump and hop
inside a simple water drop.

Impossible! Most Dutchmen said.
This Anton's crazy in the head.
We ought to ship him off to Spain.
He says he's seen a housefly's brain.
He says the water that we drink
Is full of bugs. He's mad, we think!

They called him *dumkopf*, which means dope.
That's how we got the microscope.

Maxine Kumin

115

My Uncle Dan

My Uncle Dan's an inventor, you may think that's very fine.
You may wish he was your Uncle instead of being mine –
If he wanted he could make a watch that bounces when it
　　drops,
He could make a helicopter out of string and bottle tops
Or any really useful thing you can't get in the shops.
　　　　But Uncle Dan has other ideas:
　　　　The bottomless glass for ginger beers,
　　　　The toothless saw that's safe for the tree,
　　　　A special word for a spelling bee
　　　　(Like Lionocerangoutangadder),
　　　　Or the roll-uppable rubber ladder,
　　　　The mystery pie that bites when it's bit –
　　　　My Uncle Dan invented it.
My Uncle Dan sits in his den inventing night and day.
His eyes peer from his hair and beard like mice from a load
　　of hay.
And does he make the shoes that will go walks without your
　　feet?
A shrinker to shrink instantly the elephants you meet?
A carver that just carves from the air steaks cooked and ready
　　to eat?

　　　　No, no, he has other intentions –
　　　　Only perfectly useless inventions:
　　　　Glassless windows (they never break),
　　　　A medicine to cure the earthquake,
　　　　The unspillable screwed-down cup,
　　　　The stairs that go neither down nor up,
　　　　The door you simply paint on a wall –
　　　　Uncle Dan invented them all.

Ted Hughes

Our corrugated iron tank

Our tank stood on a crazy stand,
Bare to the burning sky,
White-hot as glares the desert sand,
And dismal to the eye.
Its lid was like a rakish hat,
The tap bent all awry
And with a drip so constant that
It almost dripped when dry.
It was a most convenient tank
Wherein most things could fall;
Where snakes came from the bush and drank,
The rabbits used to call,
The mice committed suicide,
The gum-leaves sank to rest,
And in it possums dropped and died
And hornets made their nest.
But stark within my memory
I see it once again
When we looked at it anxiously –
Days when we hoped for rain;
I hear the hollow sounds it made,
Like some prophetic drum,
As I tapped rung on rung, afraid
Of dreadful days to come.
When mother in despair would pray
As low the water sank:
Four rungs, three rungs, two rungs and, aye,
How miserly we drank;
And there was none for face or hands,
Waste was a wicked thing,
There in the baked and parching lands,
With hope our only spring.
Next came the fatal 'One rung left!'
(How cruel words can be!)
As we all stood of joys bereft,
Dumb in our misery:

And then I tapped the tank in pain –
Those knells of drought and doom:
Our tank at last gone dry again,
Our home cast down in gloom;
But, oh, the joy that filled our hearts
When came the bounteous rain
And the drain-pipe sang in fits and starts
And filled the tank again!

James Hackston

Jonathan Bing Does Arithmetic

When Jonathan Bing was young, they say,
He slipped his school and ran away;
Sat in the meadow and twiddled his thumbs
And never learnt spelling or grammar or sums.

So now if you tell him, 'Add one to two,'
'Explain what you mean,' he'll answer you,
'Do you mean 2-morrow or that's 2 bad?
And what sort of 1 do you want me to add?

'For there's 1 that was first when the race was 1,
(For he ran 2 fast for the rest to run).
But if 2 had 1 when the race was through,
I'd say your answer was 1 by 2.'

'Oh Jonathan Bing, you haven't the trick
Of doing a sum in arithmetic.'
'Oh give me a chance, just one more try,'
Says Jonathan Bing with a tear in his eye.

'Very well, Jonathan, try once more,
Add up a hundred and seventy-four.'
'A hundred, and seventy-four,' says he,
'Why – that's a great age for a person to be!'

Beatrice Curtis Brown

The Twins

In form and feature, face and limb,
    I grew so like my brother,
That folks got taking me for him,
    And each for one another.
It puzzled all our kith and kin,
    It reached a fearful pitch,
For one of us was born a twin,
    Yet not a soul knew which.

One day (to make the matter worse),
    Before our names were fixed,
As we were being washed by nurse,
    We got completely mixed;
And thus you see, by Fate's decree,
    (Or rather nurse's whim),
My brother John got christened *me*,
    And I got christened *him*.

This fatal likeness even dogged
    My footsteps when at school,
And I was always getting flogged,
    For John turned out a fool.
I put this question hopelessly
    To everyone I knew –
'What *would* you do, if you were me,
    To prove that you were *you*?'

Our close resemblance turned the tide
    Of my domestic life;
For somehow my intended bride
    Became my brother's wife.
In short, year after year, the same
    Absurd mistakes went on;
And when I died – the neighbours came
    And buried brother John!

Henry S. Leigh

My Sister Jane

And I say nothing – no, not a word
About our Jane. Haven't you heard?
She's a bird, a bird, a bird, a bird.
Oh it never would do to let folks know
My sister's nothing but a great big crow.

Each day (we daren't send her to school)
She pulls on stockings of thick blue wool
To make her pin crow legs look right,
Then fits a wig of curls on tight,

And dark spectacles – a huge pair
To cover her very crowy stare.
Oh it never would do to let folks know
My sister's nothing but a great big crow.

When visitors come she sits upright
(With her wings and her tail tucked out of sight).
They think her queer but extremely polite.
Then when the visitors have gone
She whips out her wings and with her wig on
Whirls through the house at the height of your head –
Duck, duck, or she'll knock you dead.
Oh it never would do to let folks know
My sister's nothing but a great big crow.

At meals whatever she sees she'll stab it –
Because she's a crow and that's a crow habit.
My mother says 'Jane! Your manners! Please!'
Then she'll sit quietly on the cheese,
Or play the piano nicely by dancing on the keys –
Oh it never would do to let folks know
My sister's nothing but a great big crow.

Ted Hughes

When you read the following poem aloud, pretend that you have a cold in the nose.

Invalid

Raid, raid, go away,
Dote cub back udtil I say
That won't be for beddy a day.

Ad wot's the good of sudlight, dow?
When I ab kept id bed,
Ad rubbed ad poulticed for the cure
The cold that's id be head?

I've beed out od the kitched lawd,
With dothing od be feet,
Ad subthig's coffig id be deck
Ad all be head's a heat.

Tell Bay to dot bake such a doise;
Dote rud the cart so hard!
For tissudt fair, just wud of us
To rud arowd the yard.

Ad wed I try to say a tale,
Or sig a little sog,
The coffig cubs idtoo be deck
Ad tickles dredful strog.

Ad wed is father cubbig obe?
He'd dot be log he said –
If this is jist a cold it bust
Be awful to be dead!

Oh, what a log, log day it is!
Ibe tired of blocks and books;
I've cowted all the ceilig lides,
I've thought of sheep ad chooks.

I've drawed a bad's face with a bo,
I've drawed a pipe to sboke;
Just wed I thought I was asleep
I wedt ad thought I woke!

Wot's the good of sudlight dow
Ad wot's the good of raid?
Ad wot's the good of eddythig
Wed all your head's a paid?

Raid, raid, go away,
Ad dote cub back udtil I say,
Ad that wote be for beddy a day.

'Furnley Maurice'

If you had lived in the last century your poems and stories would have been very different from those you enjoy today. In Victorian times it was considered essential that children's reading should be instructive and improving, and that every verse and story should be a little sermon containing a caution or a moral.

Today we have a different attitude to life, and are inclined to parody (that is, to 'send up') the old-fashioned pedantic verses. Hilaire Belloc, Ted Hughes, Harry Graham and other poets delight in writing 'Cautionary Tales' full of ridiculous situations and hair-raising punishments for disobedient actions.

The first poem in the next group, written by Ann Taylor in 1804, should be read very seriously. The other poems are 'send-ups', so you can over-act as much as you like.

Ball

'My good little fellow, don't throw your ball
    there,
  You'll break neighbor's windows, I know:
On the end of the house there is room, and to
    spare,
Go round, you can have a delightful game there.
  Without fearing for where you may throw.'

Harry thought he might safely continue his play
  With a little more care than before;
So, heedless of all that his father could say,
As soon as he saw he was out of the way
  Resolved to have fifty throws more.

Already as far as to forty he rose,
  And no mischief had happened at all;
One more, and one more, he successfully
    throws,
But when, as he thought, just arrived at the
    close,
  In popped his unfortunate ball.

'I'm sure that I thought, and I did not intend,'
  Poor Harry was going to say;
But soon came the glazier the window to mend,
And both the bright shillings he wanted to
    spend
  He had for his folly to pay.

When little folks think they know better than
    great,
  And what is forbidden them, do,
We must always expect to see, sooner or late,
That such wise little fools have a similar fate,
  And that one in the fifty goes through.

Ann Taylor

Adventures of Isabel

Isabel met an enormous bear,
Isabel, Isabel, didn't care;
The bear was hungry, the bear was ravenous,
The bear's big mouth was cruel and cavernous.
The bear said, Isabel, glad to meet you,
How do, Isabel, now I'll eat you!
Isabel, Isabel, didn't worry,
Isabel didn't scream or scurry.
She washed her hands and she straightened her hair
    up,
Then Isabel quietly ate the bear up.

Once in a night as black as pitch
Isabel met a wicked old witch.
The witch's face was cross and wrinkled,
The witch's gums with teeth were sprinkled.
Ho ho, Isabel! the old witch crowed,
I'll turn you into an ugly toad!
Isabel, Isabel, didn't worry,
Isabel didn't scream or scurry,
She showed no rage and she showed no rancour,
But she turned the witch into milk and drank her.

Isabel met a hideous giant,
Isabel continued self-reliant.
The giant was hairy, the giant was horrid,
He had one eye in the middle of his forehead.
Good morning Isabel, the giant said,
I'll grind your bones to make my bread.
Isabel, Isabel, didn't worry,
Isabel didn't scream or scurry.
She nibbled the zwieback that she always fed off,
And when it was gone, she cut the giant's head off.

Isabel met a troublesome doctor,
He punched, and he poked till he really shocked her.
The doctor's talk was of coughs and chills
And the doctor's satchel bulged with pills.
The doctor said unto Isabel,
Swallow this, it will make you well.
Isabel, Isabel, didn't worry,
Isabel didn't scream or scurry.
She took those pills from the pill concocter,
And Isabel calmly cured the doctor.

Ogden Nash

Little Thomas

Thomas was a little glutton
Who took four times beef or mutton,
Then undid a lower button
      And consumed plum-duff,
And when he could scarcely swallow
Asked if there was more to follow,
As he'd still a tiny hollow
      That he'd like to stuff.

He was told: 'You won't get thinner
While you will eat so much dinner;
If you don't take care, some inner
      Part of you will burst.'
He replied: 'What does it matter
Even if I do get fatter?
Pure more pudding on my platter:
      Let it do its worst.'

Then one day, and little wonder,
There was a report like thunder:
Doors and windows flew asunder,
    And the cat had fits.
As his anxious friends foreboded,
Dangerously overloaded
Thomas had at length exploded,
    And was blown to bits.

His old nurse cried, much disgusted,
'There, just when I've swept and dusted,
Drat the boy! he's gone and busted,
    Making such a mess';
While the painful task of peeling
Thomas off the walls and ceiling
Gave his family a feeling
    Of sincere distress.

When a boy, who so obese is,
Scatters into tiny pieces,
And the cause of his decease is
    Having overdined,
It is hard to send a version
Of the facts of his dispersion
To the papers for insertion
    Which will be refined.

Any sorrowing relation
Asked for an elucidation
Of the awful detonation
    Was obliged to say:
'Germans have not been to bomb us:
It was only little Thomas,
Who, alas! departed from us
    In that noisy way.'

F. Gwynne Evans

Science for the Young

Thoughtful little Willie Frazer
Carved his name with father's razor;
Father, unaware of trouble,
Used the blade to shave his stubble.
Father cut himself severely,
Which pleased little Willie dearly –
'I have fixed my father's razor
So it cuts!' said Willie Frazer.

Mamie often wondered why
Acids trouble alkali –
Mamie, in a manner placid,
Fed the cat boracic acid,
Whereupon the cat grew frantic,
Executing many an antic,
'Ah!' cried Mamie, overjoyed,
'Pussy is an alkaloid!'

Arthur with a lighted taper
Touched the fire to grandpa's paper.
Grandpa leaped a foot or higher,
Dropped the sheet and shouted 'Fire!'
Arthur, wrapped in contemplation,
Viewed the scene of conflagration.
'This,' he said, 'confirms my notion –
Heat creates both light and motion.'

Wee, experimental Nina
Dropped her mother's Dresden china
From a seventh-story casement,
Smashing, crashing to the basement.
Nina, somewhat apprehensive,
Said: 'This china is expensive,
Yet it proves by demonstration
Newton's law of gravitation.'

Wallace Irwin

Sarah Cynthia Sylvia Stout

Sarah Cynthia Sylvia Stout
would not take the garbage out!
She'd boil the water
and open the cans
and scrub the pots
and scour the pans
and grate the cheese
and shell the peas
and mash the yams
and spice the hams,
and make the jams.
But though her daddy
would scream and shout,
she would not take the garbage out.
And so it piled up to the ceilings:
Coffee grounds, potato peelings,
mouldy bread and withered greens,
olive pits and soggy beans,
cracker boxes, chicken bones,
clamshells, eggshells, stale scones,
sour milk and mushy plums,
crumbly cake and cookie crumbs.
At last the garbage piled so high
that finally it reached the sky.
And none of her friends
would come to play.
And all the neighbours moved away.
And finally Sarah Cynthia Stout
said, 'I'll take the garbage out!'
But then, of course, it was too late.
The garbage reached beyond the state,
from Memphis to the Golden Gate.
And Sarah met an awful fate,
which I cannot right now relate
because the hour is much too late.

But, children, think of Sarah Stout
and always take the garbage out!

Shelley Silverstein

The Revolving Door

This is the horrible tale of Paul
MacGregor James D. Cuthbert Hall,
Who left his home one winter's day
To go to work, and on his way
In manner that was strange and weird
Mysteriously disappeared.
He left no clue, he left no trace,
He seemed to vanish into space.
Now listen to the fate of Paul
MacGregor James D. Cuthbert Hall.

He worked, did James, as shipping clerk
For Parkinson, McBaine & Burke,
Who in their store on North Broadway
Sold dry goods in a retail way.
And at the entrance to their store
There was a large revolving door
Through which passed all who went to work
For Parkinson, McBaine & Burke.

Upon this day, accursed of fate,
MacGregor James, arriving late
Dashed headlong madly toward the store,
And plunged in through the spinning door.
Around about it twirled and whirled
And Paul was twisted, curled and hurled,
And mashed, and crashed, and dashed and bashed,
As round and round it spun and flashed.

At times it nearly stopped, and then
It straightway started up again.
'I fear that I'll be late for work,
And Parkinson, McBaine & Burke
Will be distressed and grieved,' thought Paul
MacGregor James D. Cuthbert Hall.

He raised his voice in frantic cry,
And tried to hail the passers-by.
He tried in vain to call a cop,
But still the door refused to stop.
And so he spins and whirls about,
And struggles madly to get out,
While friends, heartbroken, search for Paul
MacGregor James D. Cuthbert Hall.

Newman Levy

from A Children's Don't

Don't tell Papa his nose is red
   As any rosebud or geranium,
Forbear to eye his hairless head
   Or criticise his cootlike cranium;
'Tis years of sorrow and of care
   Have made his head come through his hair.

Don't ask your uncle why he's fat;
   Avoid upon his toe-joints treading;
Don't hide a hedgehog in his hat,
   He will not see the slightest sport
In pepper put into his port!

Don't pull away the cherished chair
   On which Mamma intended sitting,
Not yet prepare her session there
   By setting on the seat her knitting;
Pause ere you hurt her spine, I pray –
   That is a game that *two* can play.

Harry Graham

*Do you know what is meant by a 'tall story'? Australians and Americans
have achieved a special reputation for telling yarns such as this one:*
   An American soldier stationed in England was boasting:
   *'At home, the winters are so cold that when we milk the cows the
milk freezes in the pails, and we have to break it up with a hammer
before we can get it out.'*
   *The Aussie soldier chipped in: 'Call that cold? Where I come from,
in the Snowy Mountains, we have to build a fire around a cow before
we can milk her.'*
   *'My uncle in the States,' persisted the American, 'has a farm nine
miles long and six miles wide. We go out to milk in the morning and
don't get home with the milk until nightfall.'*
   *'Call that big?' scoffed the Australian. 'Listen, mate. On my uncle's
farm he engages newly-married couples to go out to do the milking –
and their children bring home the milk!'*
   Collect tall stories and hold a 'yarn session' during a class period.

The Walloping Window-Blind

A capital ship for an ocean trip
  Was *The Walloping Window-Blind*;
No gale that blew dismayed her crew
  Or troubled the captain's mind.
The man at the wheel was taught to feel
  Contempt for the wildest blow,
And it often appeared, when the weather had cleared,
  That he'd been in his bunk below.

The boatswain's mate was very sedate,
  Yet fond of amusement, too;
And he played hop-scotch with the starboard watch
  While the captain tickled the crew.
And the gunner we had was apparently mad,
  For he sat on the after-rail,
And fired salutes with the captain's boots,
  In the teeth of the booming gale.

The captain sat in a commodore's hat,
  And dined, in a royal way,
On toasted pigs and pickles and figs
  And gummery bread, each day.
But the cook was Dutch, and behaved as such;
  For the food that he gave the crew
Was a number of tons of hot-cross buns,
  Chopped up with sugar and glue.

And we all felt ill as mariners will,
  On a diet that's cheap and rude;
And we shivered and shook as we dipped the cook
  In a tub of his gluesome food.

Then nautical pride we laid aside,
  And we cast the vessel ashore
On the Gulliby Isles, where the Poohpooh smiles,
  And the Anagazanders roar.

Composed of sand was that favoured land,
   And trimmed with cinnamon straws;
And pink and blue was the pleasing hue
   Of the Tickletoeteaser's claws.
And we sat on the edge of a sandy ledge
   And shot at the whistling bee;
And the Binnacle-bats wore water-proof hats
   As they danced in the sounding sea.

On rubagrub bark, from dawn to dark,
   We fed, till we all had grown
Uncommonly shrunk – when a Chinese junk
   Came by from the torriby zone.
She was stubby and square, but we didn't much care,
   And we cheerily put to sea;
And we left the crew of the junk to chew
   The bark of the rubagrub tree.

Charles Edward Carryl

137

The Crocodile

Now listen you landsmen unto me, to tell you the truth
    I'm bound,
What happened to me by going to sea, and the wonders
    that I found;
Shipwrecked I was once off Perouse and cast upon the shore,
So then I did resolve to roam, the country to explore.
'Twas far I had not scouted out, when close alongside the
    ocean,
I saw something move which at first I thought was all the
    world in motion;
But steering close alongside it, I found 'twas a crocodile,
And from his nose to the tip of his tail he measured five
    hundred mile.
While up aloft the wind was high, it blew a gale from the
    south,
I lost my hold and away did fly right into the crocodile's
    mouth,
He quickly closed his jaws on me and thought he'd got a
    victim,
But I ran down his throat, d'ye see, and that's the way I
    tricked him.
I travelled on for a month or two, till I got into his maw,
Where I found of rum-kegs not a few, and a thousand fat
    bullocks in store.
Of life I banished all my care, for of grub I was not stinted,
And in this crocodile I lived ten years, and very well
    contented.
This crocodile being very old, one day, alas, he died;
He was ten long years a-getting cold, he was so long and
    wide.
His skin was eight miles thick, I'm sure, or very near about,
For I was full ten years or more a-cutting my way out.
And now I've once more got on earth, I've vow'd no more
    to roam,
In a ship that passed I got a berth, and now I'm safe at home.

And if my story you should doubt, should ever you travel
    the Nile,
It's ten to one you'll find the shell of the wonderful crocodile.

Anon.

That *Was* a Flood

'Y'd think be the papers,' the old hand sneered,
'They was havin' a flood outback,
With their "Trains Held Up" an' "Losses Feared"
An' their screamin' headline tack.
There's maybe a trickle o' water about
Where previous no water was seen,
But I bet it ain't like when the Murray broke out
In the summer of Seventeen.

'Steamers was bushed from the source t' the mouth,
An' towns in the tops of the trees,
They stopped railin' sheep t' the markets down south,
'Cos they found they could swim them with ease.
The cod got corns on the ends of their fins
Through swimmin' from Louth to Coreen,
And whalers was washed from their boots t' their chins
In the summer of Seventeen.

'She was ten fathoms deep from the bed t' the crest;
At Echuca she's ninety mile wide.
She filled Riverina from east t' the west
An' then she poured over the side.
We went many months without seein' dry ground;
Our whiskers grew long an' turned green.
Every pub in the land was empty an' drowned
In the summer of Seventeen.

'It's clear from the papers,' the old hand declared,
As slowly his bluchers he shed,
'That a few drops o' water has got 'em all scared;
It makes me feel happy instead.'
He drew off his footwear and said, 'Now y' know
When I talks about floods what I mean:
I've had them webs what y' see on each toe
Since the summer o' Seventeen.'

Charles Shaw

Translation of the first jingle: As I went up the hill-slope I met a fox carrying away my lamb. If I had had my gun I'd never have let the fox get my lamb.

Translation of the second nonsense verse at the beginning of chapter 6: As I went up my garden path I saw my pig eating my potatoes. Oh! If I had had my stick with me I would have given that pig a whack for eating my potatoes.

7   Picture Writing

The Door

Go and open the door.
   Maybe outside there's
   a tree, or a wood,
   a garden,
   or a magic city.

Go and open the door.
   Maybe a dog's rummaging.
   Maybe you'll see a face,
or an eye,
or the picture
      of a picture.

Go and open the door.
   If there's a fog
   it will clear.

Go and open the door.
   Even if there's only
   the darkness ticking,
   even if there's only
   the hollow wind,
   even if
     nothing
       is there,
go and open the door.

At least
there'll be
a draught.

Miroslav Holub

Try your skill as a critic. Here are five pairs of statements. One of each pair was written by a craftsman skilled in writing, the other by someone who lacked the ability to make his observations come alive. Which pictures do you think were created by the more skilled writers?

An old fence was staggering down the road.
A dilapidated fence separated the garden from the road.

Birds flew from one tree to another.
Birds were arrowing from tree to tree.

Dark-hued pansies began to open.
Pansies showed their bad-tempered little faces.

A saucy little road skipped off into the hills in search of adventure.
A road wound over the hills into the distance.

A motor-bike sped off noisily in the night.
A motor-bike hammered nails of sound into the darkness.

You will have noticed that the writer who made the greater impression on you was the one who saw something through his own eyes, and helped us, by the way he used his words, to see the picture he saw or hear the sound he heard.

The poet Robert Fitzgerald saw the summer sun, and a comparison flashed into his mind: how like a warm, ripe, glowing peach it looked! Here are his own words:

> Now the sun hangs plump and high
> From the branches of the sky,
> Ripe and ready for your hand
> Could you reach it where you stand.

You must often have seen a big red summer moon. Would you have seen the same image as T. E. Hulme did when he:

> Saw the ruddy moon lean over a hedge
> Like a red-faced farmer!

143

Your garden hose is an everyday object to you but the imagination of the poet, Beatrice Janosco, makes it much more startling.

The Garden Hose

In the gray evening
I see a long green serpent
With its tail in the dahlias.

It lies in loops across the grass
And drinks softly at the faucet.

I can hear it swallow.

Beatrice Janosco

Another poet, Thomas Bailey Aldrich, watching the last leaves of gold falling from an almost bare tree, thought:

October turned my maple's leaves to gold;
The most are gone now; here and there one lingers.
Soon these will slip from out the twig's weak hold,
Like coins between a dying miser's fingers.

To the prosaic, unimaginative observer there is nothing remarkable about the humble broad bean, or an acorn, or a piece of thistledown. But how does a poet see things like this? Read 'Seeds' and see.

Seeds

A row of pearls
Delicate green
Cased in white velvet –
The broad bean.

Smallest of birds
Winged and brown,
Seed of the maple
Flutters down.

Cupped like an egg
Without a yolk,
Grows the acorn,
Seed of the oak.

Autumn the housewife
Now unlocks
Seed of the poppy
In their spice-box.

Silver hair
From an old man's crown
Wind stolen
Is thistle-down.

James Reeves

James Kirkup gives us a vivid picture of a scarecrow in a field. But he does much more – his images bring the picture to life.

The Lonely Scarecrow

My poor old bones – I've only two –
A broomshank and a broken stave,
My ragged gloves are a disgrace,
My one peg-foot is in the grave.

I wear the labourer's old clothes;
Coat, shirt and trousers all undone.
I bear my cross upon a hill
In rain and shine, in snow and sun.

I cannot help the way I look.
My funny hat is full of hay.
– O, wild birds, come and nest in me!
Why do you always fly away?

James Kirkup

Try an experiment for yourself. When you read each of the phrases in the list below, what images come to your mind? (At the end of the list we will tell you the images that other writers saw; but try not to look at these until you have written down the picture that you yourself saw.)

Butterflies flying.
Autumn leaves being blown in the wind.
Dandelions in green paddocks.
A tiny baby's hands.
Brown paper chocolate cases falling from a box.
Thunder rumbling.
A parking meter that has not expired.
New fronds of bracken fern.
A big dog's mouth.

Now look at the images that flashed into the minds of other writers, and compare them with your own.

Butterflies fluttering their stained-glass windows.
Autumn leaves turning cart-wheels on the lawn.
Green meadows pinned down with dandelion brooches.
A baby's starfish hands.
Brown parachutes floated in the air when Mother knocked
    over her box of chocolates.
Giant Thunder striding home.
A parking meter with time on its hands.
Ferns done up in pin curls.
My alsatian's mouth is a red cave.

Sometimes by a vivid word or by the combination of word and picture a writer can convey an idea or create an atmosphere so realistically that we whose senses are not as alert as his are helped to share his experience. What pictures do you see when you read these statements?

A stone splintered the sheet of glassy water.
An early bird tossed a few notes from the nest.
A fireplace glowed its greetings.
A plane winked its way into the airport.
The little village was going to sleep, window by window.

*If your Art teacher asked the class to paint a picture to capture the
spirit of a circus, he would be very disappointed if every one of you
produced the same painting. He would want to see what the circus meant
to you, personally, and he would expect that each pupil would depict
a different aspect of the 'big top'. Some pictures would show the acts –
the trapeze artists, the clowns, the acrobats; some would show the
animals in their cages, or performing in the ring; others would catch
the confusion of colour and movement of crowds, the band, the coloured
lights and the striped tents. In the same way, although several poets
may write about the one subject, each will create his own individual
picture, as you will see when you read the poems that follow.*

from The Forsaken Merman

Sand-strewn caverns, cool and deep,
Where the winds are all asleep;
Where the spent lights quiver and gleam,
Where the salt weed sways in the stream;
Where the sea-beasts, ranged all round,
Feed in the ooze of their pasture ground;
Where the sea-snakes coil and twine,
Dry their mail and bask in the brine;
Where great whales come sailing by,
Sail and sail, with unshut eye,
Round the world for ever and aye.

Matthew Arnold

The Sea

The sea is a hungry dog,
Giant and grey.
He rolls on the beach all day.
With his clashing teeth and shaggy jaws
Hour upon hour he gnaws
The rumbling, tumbling stones,
And 'Bones, bones, bones, bones!'
The giant sea-dog moans,
Licking his greasy paws.

And when the night wind roars
And the moon rocks in the stormy cloud,
He bounds to his feet and snuffs and sniffs,
Shaking his wet sides over the cliffs,
And howls and hollos long and loud.

But on quiet day in May or June,
When even the grasses on the dune
Play no more their reedy tune,
With his head between his paws
He lies on the sandy shores,
So quiet, so quiet, he scarcely snores.

James Reeves

from Green Lions

The bay is gouged by the wind.
In the jagged hollows green lions crouch
And stretch
And slouch
And sudden with spurting manes and a glitter
    of haunches
Charge at the shore
And rend the sand and roar.

Douglas Stewart

Although a painting may hang motionless on your wall it is possible to see movement in it; for the skilful artist can convey a feeling of action. In his landscape the gale tosses the trees; clouds tumble across the sky; people lashed by rain and hail force their way against the wind with heads down and coat collars turned up. The writer, too, by his use of vigorous words, can make a printed page pulsate with movement and sound. Notice how Stephen Crane has captured the clamour and commotion of the fair-ground in this prose paragraph:

from The Pace of Youth

Within the Merry-Go-Round there was a whirling circle of ornamental lions, giraffes, camels, ponies, goats ... With stiff wooden legs they swept on in a never-ending race, while a great orchestrion clamored in wild speed ... A host of laughing children bestrode the animals, bending forward like charging cavalrymen, shaking reins and whooping in glee ... Occasionally a father might arise and go near to shout encouragement, cautionary commands, or applause at his flying offspring. Frequently mothers called out 'Be careful, Georgie!' The orchestrion bellowed and thundered on its platform, filling the ears with its long monotonous song. Over in a corner, a man in a white apron behind a counter roared above the tumult: 'Popcorn! Popcorn!'

Stephen Crane

The Main Deep

The long-rolling,
Steady-pouring,
Deep-trenched
Green billow:
The wide-topped,
Unbroken,
Green-glacid,
Slow-sliding,
Cold-flushing
– On – on – on –
Chill-rushing,
Hush – hushing
. . . Hush – hushing . . .

James Stephens

What are your own feelings about the sea? Try to express them in writing. Perhaps these images may spark off your imagination:

A storm of seagulls swept over the water.
The gentle sea was spreading white lace on the shore.
Small waves were chucking dinghies under the chin.
The many-twinkling smile of ocean.
A row-boat was scratching its chin on the beach.

The following poems are poems of action.

Gale Warning

The wind breaks bound, tossing the oak and chestnut,
Whirling the paper at street corners,
The city clerks are harassed, wrestling head-down:
The gulls are blown inland.

Three slates fall from a roof,
The promenade is in danger:
Inland, the summer fête is postponed,
The British glider record broken.

The wind blows through the City, cleansing,
Whipping the posters from the hoardings,
Tearing the bunting and the banners,
The wind blows steadily, and as it will.

Michael Roberts

A Windy Day

This wind brings all dead things to life,
Branches that lash the air like whips
And dead leaves rolling in a hurry
Or peering in a rabbits' bury
Or trying to push down a tree;
Gates that fly open to the wind
And close again behind,
And fields that are a flowing sea
And make the cattle look like ships;
Straws glistening and stiff
Lying on air as on a shelf,

And pond that leaps to leave itself;
And feathers too that rise and float,
Each feather changed into a bird,
And line-hung sheets that crack and strain;
Even the sun-greened coat,
That through so many winds has served,
The scarecrow struggles to put on again.

Andrew Young

Flying

I saw the moon,
One windy night,
Flying so fast –
All silvery white –
Over the sky
Like a toy balloon
Loose from its string –
A runaway moon.
The frosty stars
Went racing past,
Chasing her on
Ever so fast.
Then everyone said,
'It's the clouds that fly,
And the stars and moon
Stand still in the sky.'
But I don't mind –
I saw the moon
Sailing away
Like a toy
Balloon.

J. M. Westrup

Wind

Grass like small feet following,
  wind-worried. Wind in Moreton Figs
  through leaves hand-broad, thick, stiff, through boughs
  soft-clumsy, loutish, knotted: wind roar-loud
  in undertones, congealed in trees, and suddenly
  shrill-free again. In pines it sings
  a high clear note in palms it creaks,
  rubs, rustles all the night: one tells what tree
  by wind-sound. In the Moreton Figs
  along the river, roar, roar, loud and deep
  and dully warped, unlovely, menacing. And grass
  like small feet following.

Peter Miles

The Song of the Sea Wind

How it sings, sings, sings,
  Blowing sharply from the sea-line,
With an edge of salt that stings;
  How it laughs aloud, and passes,
As it cuts the close cliff-grasses;
  How it sings again, and whistles
As it shakes the stout sea-thistles –
  How it sings!

How it shrieks, shrieks, shrieks,
  In the crannies of the headlands
In the gashes of the creeks;
  How it shrieks once more, and catches
Up the yellow foam in patches:
  How it whirls it out and over
To the corn-field and the clover –
  How it shrieks!

How it roars, roars, roars,
   In the iron under-caverns,
In the hollows of the shores;
   How it roars anew, and thunders,
As the strong hull splits and sunders:
   And the spent ship, tempest driven,
On the reef lies rent and riven –
   How it roars!

How it wails, wails, wails,
   In the tangle of the wreckage,
In the flapping of the sails;
   How it sobs away, subsiding,
Like a tired child after chiding;
   And across the ground-swell rolling,
You can hear the bell-buoy tolling –
   How it wails!

                              Austin Dobson

A Piper

A piper in the streets to-day
Set up, and tuned, and started to play,
And away, away, away on the tide
Of his music we started; on every side
Doors and windows were opened wide,
And men left down their work and came,
And women with petticoats coloured like flame,
And little bare feet that were blue with cold,
Went dancing back to the age of gold,
And all the world went gay, went gay,
For half an hour in the street to-day.

                              Seumas O'Sullivan

from Clipper Ships

Beautiful as a tiered cloud, skysails set and shrouds twanging,
she emerges from the surges that keep running away before
day on the low Pacific shore. With the roar of the wind
blowing half a gale, she heels and lunges, and buries her
bows in the smother, lifting them swiftly, and scattering the
glistening spray-drops from her jib-sails with laughter...

John Gould Fletcher

*Have you ever listened to a piece of music in which the musician has
blended his notes so harmoniously that a feeling of tranquillity comes
over you? A writer can make you feel the same serenity, as you will
see in the next poems. Try to find recordings of* Claire de Lune, The
Swan, La Mer *or other 'peaceful' music that you could use as accom-
paniment to class reading.*

The Swans

How lovely are these swans,
That float like high proud galleons
Cool in the summer heat,
And waving leaf-like feet
Divide with narrow breasts of snow
In a smooth surge
This water that is mostly sky;
So lovely that I know
Death cannot kill such birds,
It could but wound them, mortally.

Andrew Young

Silver

Slowly, silently, now the moon
Walks the night in her silver shoon;
This way, and that, she peers, and sees
Silver fruit upon silver trees;
One by one the casements catch
Her beams beneath the silvery thatch;
Couched in his kennel, like a log,
With paws of silver sleeps the dog;
From their shadowy cote the white breasts peep
Of doves in silver-feathered sleep;
A harvest mouse goes scampering by,
With silver claws, and silver eye;
And moveless fish in the water gleam,
By silver reeds in a silver stream.

Walter de la Mare

159

Just as colour TV has brought a new dimension into our lives, so many poets arouse our senses by making their descriptions glow with colour and light.

Fireworks

They rise like sudden fiery flowers
    That burst upon the night,
Then fall to earth in burning showers
    Of crimson, blue, and white.

Like buds too wonderful to name,
    Each miracle unfolds,
And catherine-wheels begin to flame
    Like whirling marigolds.

Rockets and Roman candles make
    An orchard of the sky,
Whence magic trees their petals shake
    Upon each gazing eye.

James Reeves

The Wasp

When the ripe pears droop heavily,
The yellow wasp hums loud and long
His hot and drowsy autumn song.
A yellow flame he seems to be,
When darting suddenly from high
He lights where fallen peaches lie.
Yellow and black – this tiny thing's
A tiger-soul on elfin wings.

William Sharp

Symphony in Yellow

An omnibus across the bridge
Crawls like a yellow butterfly,
And, here and there, a passer-by
Shows like a little restless midge.

Big barges full of yellow hay
Are moored against the shadowy wharf,
And, like a yellow silken scarf,
The thick fog hangs along the quay.

The yellow leaves begin to fade
And flutter from the Temple elms,
And at my feet the pale green Thames
Lies like a rod of rippled jade.

Oscar Wilde

from September, 1918

This afternoon was the colour of water falling through
    sunlight;
The trees glittered with the tumbling of leaves;
The sidewalks shone like alleys of dropped maple leaves,
And the houses ran along them laughing out of square,
    open windows.
Under a tree in the park,
Two little boys, lying flat on their faces,
Were carefully gathering red berries
To put in a pasteboard box.

Amy Lowell

from Ombre Chinoise

Red foxgloves against a yellow wall streaked with plum-
    coloured shadows;
A lady with a blue and red sunshade;
The slow dash of waves upon a parapet.
That is all.

Amy Lowell

The Lights

I know the ships that pass by day:
I guess their business, grave or gay,
    And spy their flags, and learn their names,
        And whence they come and where they go –
        But in the night I only know
Some little starry flames.

And yet I think these jewelled lights
Have meanings full as noonday sights;
    That every emerald signs to me
        That ship and souls are harbour near,
        And every ruby rich and clear
Proclaims them bound for sea.

And all the yellow diamonds set
On mast and deck and hull in jet
    Have meanings real as day can show:
        They tell of care, of watchful eyes,
        Of labour, slumber, hopes, and sighs –
Of human joy and woe.

O ships that come and go by night,
God's blessing be on every light!

J. J. Bell

Shining Things

I love all shining things –
    the lovely moon, ← rhyme
The silver stars at night,
    gold sun at noon.
A glowing rainbow in
    a stormy sky,
Or bright clouds hurrying ← Personification
    when wind goes by.

I love the glow-worm's elf-light
    in the lane,
And leaves a-shine with glistening
    drops of rain,
The glinting wings of bees,
    and butterflies,
My purring pussy's green
    and shining eyes.

I love the street-lamps shining
    through the gloom,
Tall candles lighted in
    a shadowy room,
New-tumbled chestnuts from
    the chestnut tree,
And gleaming fairy bubbles
    blown by me.

I love the shining buttons
    on my coat,
I love the bright beads round ← necklace
    my mother's throat.
I love the coppery flames
    of red and gold,
That cheer and comfort me
    when I'm a-cold.

163

The beauty of all shining things
           is yours and mine,
It was a *lovely* thought of God
           to make things shine.

Elizabeth Gould

from Day of the Kingfisher

Look! Look! See, the kingfisher comes –
There where the white log splits the pool.
O the blue flash of him like from a thundercloud!
See, there he goes – over the rockfall.
Now where the banksias on the creek's elbow
Lean scarlet to scarlet – O how he flashes!
Look, look – ah, he is gone.

Yet for his coming the laurel more vibrant,
Bolder the bronze of young leaf on the fig,
And softer too the gloom-thought green of sheoak.
How all things now are lovelier since he came!

Paul L. Grano

Magic

Crawling up the hillside,
Swinging round the bay,
With a ceaseless humming
Ply the trams all day.

When it's dark I linger
Just to see the sight,
All those jewelled beetles
Flashing through the night!

Anything more lovely
I have never seen
Than the sparks above them,
White and blue and green;

Sometimes they are tiny:
In a storm they shine,
Dragons' tongues that follow
All along the line!

When the wind has fallen
And the bay's like glass,
Would you see some magic?
Watch what comes to pass:

There is just a ripple
Where the water breaks,
All the lamps reflected
Show like golden snakes:

Wait, the tram is coming
Round the curving shore,
And its humming changes
To a hollow roar:

There's a flaming glory
On the bay at last,
Red and green and orange –
It has come, and passed . . .

Nothing breaks the stillness,
All is as before,
And the golden serpents
Quiver near the shore . . .

Trams are only ugly
Passing day by day,
But at night their crudeness
Vanishes away.

Some kind of magic clothes them
In a fairer dress,
So that we may wonder
At their loveliness!

Dorothea Mackellar

Things to do
Dorothea Mackellar is fascinated by the way the commonplace, rather ugly trams are transformed by lights. Describe a scene that becomes a thing of magic at night. (Compare Luna Park in the daylight and at night; think of the airport at night; remember the difference when the lights on the Christmas tree were lit. . . . You will have many other ideas.)

Oscar Wilde's 'Symphony in Yellow' is a London scene. Try to write an Australian 'Symphony in Gold' or a 'Symphony in Green.'

Snow country

only
a little
yellow

school bus
creeping along
a thin

ribbon
of snow road
splashed colour

on the white
winter canvas
that was

Wyoming
from the train
yesterday

David Etter

So far we have discussed things that we see – pictures, movement, colour and light. But we have many other senses that sharpen our enjoyment of life. Read these two descriptions and see whether the author's words have made your mouth water:

from Stina, the Story of a Cook

How we ate of Stina's home-made sausage, eggs fried in rosemary butter, apple pancakes dripping with buckwheat honey, and winding up with a tart made of raised sweet dough, filled with thick cream, dotted with yellow plums dusted with sugar and cinnamon.

Herman Smith

from Here's England

The gingerbread smelt heavenly, all spicy, hot and brown, with waxy sticky wells of the spice where I'd dropped in the ginger and the cloves.

Dorothy Hartley

R. C. Hutchinson brings us the good country smells *when he describes the wind which*

... bore damp odours, as the autumn wind had, but of a homelier kind; not of the high bogs and salty, mountain mists, but of water trickling through stone and moss, of valley ferns and faintly, with the farmyard smells from Randall's Gift, of cowslip and hyacinth.

R. C. Hutchinson

Then we distinguish things by their feel, by using our sense of touch. John Burroughs has recaptured in words the feel of the apples in his orchard.

from Winter Sunshine

Is there any other fruit that has so much facial expression as the apple? ... There is not only the size and shape, but there is the texture, and polish. Some apples are coarse-grained and some are fine; some are thin-skinned and some are thick. One variety is quick and vigorous beneath the touch, another gentle and yielding. The pinnock has a thick skin with a spongy lining; a bruise in it becomes like a piece of cork. The tallow apple has an unctuous feel ... It sheds water like a duck ... Some varieties impress me as masculine – weather-stained, freckled, lasting and rugged; others are indeed lady apples, fair, delicate, shining, mild-flavoured, white mealed ... The practised hand knows each kind.

John Burroughs

Do you think that Rupert Brooke has succeeded in conveying the feel of things when he writes of
 the cool kindliness of sheets, that soon
 Smooth away trouble; and the rough male kiss
 Of blankets.

'I like noise,' claims a poet, and goes on to list the lively sounds that make up the everyday music of her life.

Noise

I like noise.
The whoop of a boy, the thud of a hoof,
The rattle of rain on a galvanised roof,
The hubbub of traffic, the roar of a train,
The throb of machinery numbing the brain,
The switching of wires in an overhead tram,
The rush of the wind, a door on the slam,
The boom of the thunder, the crash of the waves,
The din of a river that races and raves,
The crack of a rifle, the clank of a pail,
The strident tattoo of a swift-slapping sail –
From any old sound that the silence destroys
Arises a gamut of soul-stirring joys.
I like noise.

Jessie Pope

The next two writers have captured the sound and movement of bees as they tumble among the heavily scented summer flowers.

Bees

You voluble,
    Velvety
Vehement fellows
That play on your
Flying and
Musical 'cellos,
All goldenly
Girdled you
Serenade clover,
Each artist in
Bass but a
Bibulous rover!
You passionate,
Powdery
Pastoral bandits,
Who gave you your
Roaming and
Rollicking mandates?
Come out of my
Foxglove; come
Out of my roses
You bees with the
Plushy and
Plausible noses!

Norman Gale

from The Pine Wood

The wasps were working at the pine boughs high overhead;
the bees by dozens were crowding to the bramble flowers;
swarming on them they seemed so delighted; bumble-bees
went wandering among the ferns in the copse and in the
ditches ... calling at every purple heath-blossom, at the
purple knapweeds, purple thistles and broad handfuls of
yellow-weed flowers.

Richard Jefferies

You be the poet.
When you go to bed tonight, lie quietly and listen. At first everything
seems silent. Then you will hear sounds: the busy tick of the alarm
clock near your bed; a laugh from the lounge room; a creak in the
ceiling; the flap of a blind; the cat padding round the house....
    Tomorrow, keeping only to the sounds you actually heard, try to
recapture them in a poem. Try to make 'sound pictures' using some of
these ideas as subjects:
    A modern jazz group
    Four o'clock. School's out!
    Rain on the roof
    Men at work (cement mixers, welders, pneumatic drills)
    Jet planes

The last poem in this section is by Kenneth Slessor, who is re-creating
the opening scene of the ballet Petroushka. *The poet takes you to the*
fairground. Here the colourful crowds, the stalls, the stall-holders all
flash past your eyes; a confusion of noise assails your ears; you are
whirled along by the rhythm of ballet until the last few lines, when
the tempo changes and the story is about to begin.

Petroushka

In and out the countryfolk, the carriages and carnival,
Pastry-cooks in all directions push to barter their confections,
Trays of little gilded cakes, caramels in painted flakes,
Marzipan of various makes and macaroons of all complex-
　ions,
Riding on a tide of country faces.

Up and down the smoke and crying,
Girls with apple-eyes are flying,
Country boys in costly braces
Run with red, pneumatic faces;
Trumpets gleam, whistles scream,
Organs cough their coloured steam out,
Dogs are worming, sniffing, squirming;
Air-balloons and paper moons,
Roundabouts with curdled tunes,
Drowned bassoons and waggon-jacks;
Tents like flowers of candle-wax;
'Buy, buy, buy, buy!'
Cotton ties, cakes and pies, what a size, test your eyes,
hair-dyes, candy-shies all a prize, penny tries,
no lies, watch it rise, Buy, buy, buy, buy!'
So everybody buys.

Gently the doctor of magic mutters.
Opens his puppet-stall,
Pulls back the painted shutters,
Ruffles the golden lace.
Ha! The crowd flutters . . .
Reddened and sharp and small,
O, *Petroushka*'s face!

Kenneth Slessor

8 Feelings and Experiences

Lament of Hsi-Chun

My people have married me
In a far corner of Earth;
Sent me away to a strange land,
To the king of the Wu-Sun.
A tent is my house,
Of felt are my walls;
Raw flesh my food
With mare's milk to drink.
Always thinking of my own country,
My heart sad within.
Would I were a yellow stork
And could fly to my old home!

Hsi-Chun (translated by Arthur Waley)

175

It is over two thousand years ago that the young Chinese girl, Hsi-Chun, was sent away from her home to be the wife of an old king; yet, today, we who are separated from her by so many centuries and so many miles can still feel the loneliness and homesickness expressed in her simple verse. We know that the young bride did not go gladly to a husband of her own choice – the words 'my people have married me' and 'sent me away' tell us this. The phrases 'far corner of Earth' and 'strange land' echo the despair of an exile far from home. When Hsi-Chun complains of eating 'raw flesh' and drinking 'mare's milk' we feel her distaste for the uncivilised ways of her husband's tribesmen. She yearns to escape from this alien way of life, and envies the yellow stork as it wings overhead – for to her it is a symbol of freedom.

Men and women are moved to write by many different kinds of feelings. The poems that you are now going to read express emotions such as despair, determination, contentment, longing and delight. In your discussion of these poems you may come to understand the poet's feelings more sympathetically if you ask yourself the questions:

What are the poet's feelings?
What has caused him to feel like this?
Which words and ideas have helped you to understand his feelings?

Boy Fishing

I am cold and alone,
On my tree-root sitting as still as stone.
The fish come to my net. I scorned the sun,
The voices on the road, and they have gone.
My eyes are buried in the cold pond, under
The cold, spread leaves; my thoughts are silver-wet.
I have ten stickleback, a half-day's plunder,
Safe in my jar. I shall have ten more yet.

E. J. Scovell

The Dunce

He says no with his head
but he says yes with his heart
he says yes to what he loves
he says no to the teacher

he stands
he is questioned
and all the problems are posed
sudden laughter seizes him
and he erases all
the words and figures
names and dates
sentences and snares
and despite the teacher's threats
to the jeers of infant prodigies
with chalk of every colour
on the blackboard of misfortune
he draws the face of happiness.

Jacques Prévert
translated by Lawrence Ferlinghetti

The Orphan

To be an orphan,
To be fated to be an orphan,
How bitter is this lot!
When my father and mother were alive
I used to ride in a carriage
With four fine horses.
But when they both died,
My brother and my sister-in-law
Sent me out to be a merchant.
In the south I travelled to the 'Nine Rivers'
And in the east as far as Ch'i and Lu.
At the end of the year when I came home
I dared not tell them what I had suffered –
Of the lice and vermin in my head,
Of the dust in my face and eyes.
My brother told me to get ready the dinner,
My sister-in-law told me to see after the horses.

I was always going up into the hall
And running down again to the parlour.
My tears fell like rain.
In the morning they sent me to draw water,
I didn't get back till night-fall,
My hands were all sore
And I had no shoes.
I walked the cold earth
Treading on thorns and brambles.
As I stopped to pull out the thorns,
How bitter my heart was!
My tears fell and fell
And I went on sobbing and sobbing.
In winter I have no great-coat;
Nor in summer thin clothes.
It is no pleasure to be alive.
I had rather quickly leave the earth
And go beneath the Yellow Springs.
The April winds blow
And the grass is growing green.
In the third month – silkworms and mulberries,
In the sixth month – the melon-harvest.
I went out with the melon-cart
And just as I was coming home
The melon-cart turned over.
The people who came to help me were few,
But the people who ate the melons were many.
'At least leave me the stalks
To take home as proof.
My brother and sister-in-law are harsh,
And will be certain to call me to account.'
When I got home, how they shouted and scolded!
I want to write a letter and send it
To my mother and father under the earth,
And tell them I can't go on any longer
Living with my brother and sister-in-law.

Unknown Chinese Poet (translated by Arthur Waley)

With Half an Eye

At seven the sun that lit my world blew out
Leaving me only mist. Through which I probed
My way to school, guessed wildly at the sums
Whose marks on the board I couldn't even see.

They wanted to send me away to a special school.
I refused, and coped as best I could with half
The light lost in the mist, screwing my tears
Into my work, my gritted teeth, my writing –

Which crawled along and writhed. Think thoughts at will,
None of it comes across. Even now friends ask
'How do you read your writing?' The fact is, I don't;
Nobody could. I guess. But how would you

Like my world where parallels actually join,
Dimensions vary at sight? Once in a pub
I walked towards a sign marked gents over
A grating and crashed through the floor –

Well, it looked all right to me. Those steep stairs
People told me of later flattened to lines
In my half-world. The rest imagination
Supplied: when you've half a line you extend it.

The lenses drag their framework down my nose.
I still can't look strangers in the face,
Wilting behind a wall of glass at them.
It makes me look shifty at interviews.

I wake up with a headache, chew all day
Aspirins, go to bed dispirited,
Still with a dull pain somewhere in my skull,
And sleep. Then, in my dreams, the sun comes out.

Philip Hobsbaum

Releasing a Migrant 'Yen' (Wild Goose)

At Nine Rivers, in the tenth year, in winter, – heavy snow;
The river-water covered with ice and the forests broken
    with their load.
The birds of the air, hungry and cold, went flying east and
    west;
And with them flew a migrant 'yen', loudly clamouring for
    food.
Among the snow it pecked for grass; and rested on the
    surface of the ice:
It tried with its wings to scale the sky; but its tired flight
    was slow.
The boys of the river spread a net and caught the bird as it
    flew;
They took it in their hands to the city-market and sold it
    there alive.
I that was once a man of the North am now an exile here:
Bird and man, in their different kind, are each strangers in
    the south.
And because the sight of an exiled bird wounded an exile's
    heart,
I paid your ransom and set you free, and you flew away to
    the clouds.

Chinese poem, translated by Arthur Waley

Where Have All the Flowers Gone?

Where have all the flowers gone?
Long time passing.
Where have all the flowers gone?
Long time ago.
Where have all the flowers gone?
Young girls have picked them every one.
O when will they ever learn?
When will they ever learn?

Where have all the young girls gone,
 Long time passing?
Where have all the young girls gone,
Long time ago?
Where have all the young girls gone?
Gone to husbands everyone.
O, when will they ever learn?
When will they ever learn?

Where have all the husbands gone?
Long time passing.
Where have all the husbands gone?
Long time ago.
Where have all the husbands gone?
Gone for soldiers every one.
O when will they ever learn?
When will they ever learn?

Where have all the soldiers gone?
Long time passing.
Where have all the soldiers gone?
Long time ago.
Where have all the soldiers gone?
Gone to graveyards everyone.
O, when will they ever learn?
When will they ever learn?

Where have all the graveyards gone?
Long time passing.
Where have all the graveyards gone?
Long time ago.
Where have all the graveyards gone?
Gone to flowers everyone.
O, when will they ever learn?
When will they ever learn?

Where have all the flowers gone?
Long time passing.
Where have all the flowers gone?
Long time ago.
Where have all the flowers gone?
Young girls have picked them everyone.
O, when will they ever learn?
When will they ever learn?

Anon.

You have probably noticed how old people love to recall times of their youth. Can you remember any of the stories your grand-parents have told you of their school-days and the towns where they lived?

In 'It was long ago' a woman tells us of an incident she will never forget. It was not particularly exciting; rather, it was something commonplace that could have happened to any of us. Yet she can still recapture the very feelings she experienced on that hot day so long ago.

In 'The Quilt' each patchwork square holds for the old lady a memory from the past.

It was Long Ago

I'll tell you, shall I, something I remember?
Something that still means a great deal to me.
It was long ago.

A dusty road in summer I remember,
A mountain, and an old house, and a tree
That stood, you know

Behind the house. An old woman I remember
In a red shawl with a grey cat on her knee
Humming under a tree.

She seemed the oldest thing I can remember,
But then perhaps I was not more than three.
It was long ago.

I dragged on the dusty road, and I remember
How the old woman looked over the fence at me
And seemed to know

How it felt to be three, and called out, I remember
'Do you like bilberries and cream for tea?'
I went under the tree

And while she hummed, and the cat purred, I remember
How she filled a saucer with berries and cream for me
So long ago,

Such berries and such cream as I remember
I never had seen before, and never see
To-day, you know.

And that is almost all I can remember,
The house, the mountain, the grey cat on her knee,
Her red shawl, and the tree,

And the taste of the berries, the feel of the sun I remember,
And the smell of everything that used to be
So long ago,

Till the heat on the road outside again I remember,
And how the long dusty road seemed to have for me
No end, you know.

That is the farthest thing I can remember.
It won't mean much to you. It does to me.
Then I grew up, you see.

Eleanor Farjeon

The Quilt

That day we said goodbye to her,
Winter at work outside, the fire-flecked room
No louder than the black cat's purr
Breathing the way to her doom,
I saw it lying, solid and smooth there,
Her patchwork quilt,
A huge and dangling square,
Triangles of white, oblongs of red,
With bits from curtain and kilt.
I thought it looked just like
A landscape of little fields, seen
In springtime from an aeroplane,
Or, with dots of orange-green,
The mottled back of some big river pike.
And there were strips of calico in that counterpane,
Flannel from a grey Welsh shirt,
A blue velvet diamond, some sprigged lawn,
Faded pieces of a gingham skirt.
And as we slowly watched the dawn
Chequering the vast and empty sky,
'That was my wedding dress' she softly said,
Placing her fingers on one silky hexagon;
She smiled, and finished with a sigh,
The fingers stiffened, the old head bowed.
Before we left, my grandmother had gone,
And married on that morning to the dead,
Lay calm and beautiful in her quilted shroud.

Leonard Clark

In the next three poems we experience a sailor's fight for life, a father's heartbreak, and a young boy's first tragedy.

When the Plane Dived

When the plane dived and the machine-gun spattered
The deck, in his numb clutch the tugging wheel
Bucked madly as he strove to keep the keel
Zig-zagging through the steep and choppy sea –
To keep zig-zagging, that was all that mattered . . .
To keep the ship zig-zagging endlessly,
Dodging that diving devil. Now again
The bullets spattered like a squall of rain
About him; and again with desperate grip
He tugged, to port the helm . . . to keep the ship
Zig-zagging . . . zagging through eternity;
To keep the ship . . . A sudden scalding pain
Shot through his shoulder and the whole sky shattered
About him in red fire; and yet his grip
Tightened upon the wheel . . . To keep the ship
Zig . . . zig . . . zig-zagging, that was all that mattered.

Wilfrid Gibson

The man who finds his son has become a thief

Coming into the store at first angry
At the accusation, believing in
The word of his boy who has told him:
I didn't steal anything, honest.

Then becoming calmer, seeing that anger
Will not help in the business, listening painfully
As the other's evidence unfolds, so painfully slow.

Then seeing gradually that evidence
Almost as if tighten slowly around the neck
Of his son, at first vaguely circumstantial, then gathering
    damage
Until there is present the unmistakable odour of guilt
Which seeps now into the mind and lays its poison.

Suddenly feeling sick and alone and afraid,
As if an unseen hand had slapped him in the face
For no reason whatsoever; wanting to get out
Into the street, the night, the darkness, anywhere to hide
The pain that must show in the face to these strangers, the
    fear.

It must be like this.
It could hardly be otherwise.

Raymond Souster

End of a Harvest Day

It was harvest time
and all farm hands were working
as hard as possible,
before the weather changed for the worse.
The tractor was pulling along
a hay cart.
The farm hands were loading the bales on to it.
Captain, the young sheep dog, was romping
about around the bales
and getting under everyone's feet,
getting in the way all the time.
It was a warm sunny day
and everybody was cheerful.
The work was hard
and soon all shirts were off.
The farmer's son began playing with Captain,
and his laughing and Captain's barking
echoed round the
silent hills.

The cart was almost loaded when
the young lad decided to get up
beside the tractor driver;
Captain stood by the wheel,
barking at him to come down.
But the young lad was enjoying himself
on the tractor.
He had edged his way along
the bonnet and was sitting
with his legs hanging down
over the grill at the front.
Captain must have thought
that the bonnet was big enough for two
He jumped –
and missed .
His front legs scraped

down the side of the tractor
Then his legs went through
the air vent.
He gave a sharp piercing yelp
and fell to the ground.

We all turned round,
to see Captain limping away.
The tractor had smashed his right front leg
and the flesh hung loose.
Except for the first yelp
he did not whimper at all.
The lad burst into tears.
And an elderly farm hand led the dog
back to the farm house.
We tried to console the boy,
but he knew as well as we did
what was going to happen.

The report was loud
and echoed for some time.
Then silence.
Although we know life is hard,
we felt a lump in our throats,
but no one admitted it.
But the day's work was finished
in silence,
without Captain's bark or the boy's laughter.

John Hurst

In this chapter we have read of feelings and experiences – the exciting, the commonplace, the individual, the shared. The last poem in the book tells the life story of a Red Indian woman of the Chippewa tribe. What are the experiences she has had, and what feelings do they arouse in you?

The Forsaken

Once in the winter
Out on a lake
In the heart of the north-land
Far from the Fort
And far from the hunters
A Chippewa woman
With her sick baby.
Crouched in the last hours
Of a great storm
Frozen and hungry,
She fished through the ice
With a line of the twisted
Bark of the cedar
And a rabbit-bone hook
Polished and barbed;
Fished with the bare hook
All through the wild day,
Fished and caught nothing;
While the young chieftain
Tugged at her breasts,
Or slept in the lacings
Of the warm tikanagan.
All the lake-surface
Streamed with the hissing
Of millions of iceflakes
Hurled by the wind;
Behind her the round
Of a lonely island
Roared like a fire
With the voice of the storm
In the deeps of the cedars.
Valiant, unshaken,
She took of her own flesh,
Baited the fish-hook,
Drew in a grey-trout,
Drew in his fellow,

Heaped them beside her,
Dead in the snow.
Valiant, unshaken,
She faced the long distance,
Wolf-haunted and lonely,
Sure of her goal
And the life of her dear one:
Tramped for two days,
On the third in the morning,
Saw the strong bulk
Of the Fort by the river,
Saw the wood-smoke
Hang soft in the spruces,
Heard the keen yelp
Of the ravenous huskies
Fighting for whitefish
Then she had rest.
Years and years after
When she was old and withered,
When her son was an old man
And his children filled with vigour
They came in their northern tour
    on the verge of winter
To an island in a lonely lake.
There one night they camped,
    and on the morrow
Gathered their kettles and
    birch-bark,
Their rabbit-skin robes and
    their mink-traps,
Launched their canoes and slunk
    away through the islands,
Left her alone forever,
Without a word of farewell,
Because she was old and useless,
Like a paddle broken and warped,
Or a pole that was splintered.

Then, with a sigh,
Valiant, unshaken,
She smoothed her dark locks
    under her kerchief,
Composed her shawl in state,
Then folded her hands ridged with
    sinews and corded with veins,
Folded them across her breasts
    spent with the nourishing of children,
Gazed at the sky past the tops of
    the cedars,
Saw two spangled nights arise out
    of the twilight,
Saw two days go by filled with
    the tranquil sunshine,
Saw, without pain, or dread, or
    even a moment of longing:
Then on the third great night there came
    thronging and thronging
Millions of snowflakes out of a
    windless cloud;
They covered her close with a
    beautiful crystal shroud.
Covered her deep and silent.
But in the frost of the dawn,
Up from the life below,
Rose a column of breath
Through a tiny cleft in the snow,
Fragile, delicately drawn,
Wavering with its own weakness,
In the wilderness a sign of the spirit,
Persisting still in the sight of the sun
Till day was done.
Then all light was gathered up by the hand of
    God and hid in His breast,
Thén there was born a silence deeper than silence,
Then she had rest.

Duncan Campbell Scott

Index of Authors

194

Acknowledgements

For permission to reprint copyright material, thanks are due to the
following: George Allen & Unwin Ltd., for 'The End of the Road'
by Hilaire Belloc from *The Path to Rome*; Angus & Robertson Ltd.,
for 'The Shepherd' by Mary Gilmore and 'Petroushka' by Kenneth
Slessor; James Nimmo Britton, for 'Space Travellers'; Jonathan Cape
Limited (and Mrs. H. M. Davies), for 'A Strange Meeting' by W. H.
Davies, and (with the trustees of the estate of Robert Frost) for 'The
Fear' by Robert Frost from *The Poetry of Robert Frost*, edited by Edward
Connery Lathem; City Lights Inc., for 'The Dunce' by Jacques Prévert;
Constable & Co. Ltd., for 'The Lament of Hsi-Chun', 'The Orphan'
and 'Releasing a Migrant "Yen"' from Arthur Waley's translation of
170 Chinese Poems; The Cresset Press Limited, for 'A Child's Dream'
by Frances Cornford from her *Collected Poems* and for 'Boy Fishing'
by E. J. Scovell from *The River Steamer*; J. M. Dent & Sons Ltd, for
'The Adventures of Isabel' by Ogden Nash from *Family Reunion*;
Gerald Duckworth & Co. Ltd., for 'The Lion and the Tiger' by Hilaire
Belloc; Evans Brothers Limited, for 'Shining Things' by Elizabeth
Gould from *Book of a Thousand Poems*; Faber & Faber Ltd, for 'Gale
Warning' by Michael Roberts from his *Collected Poems* and for 'My
Sister Jane' and 'My Uncle Dan' from *Meet My Folks* by Ted Hughes;
Donald Finkel, for 'The Hunting Song'; The executors of Mrs Hamilton
Fyfe and the Barnisdale Press, for 'Men are Like Cats' by Mary Carn;
Georgian House Pty Ltd., for 'Day of the Kingfisher' by Paul L. Grano;
Granada Publishing Co., for 'The Quilt' by Leonard Clark; Sir Alexander
Gray, for 'On a Cat, Ageing'; Harcourt, Brace and World Inc., for
'Dog at Night' by Louis Untermeyer from *The Long Feud: Selected
Poems*, © 1928 by Harcourt, Brace and World Inc., renewed 1956 by
Louis Untermeyer; Harper & Row, for 'Sarah Cynthia Sylvia Stout'
by Shelley Silverstein; George C. Harrap & Co. Ltd., for 'The Fugitive'
by Dorothy Stuart from *Historical Songs and Ballads*; Rupert Hart-Davis
Limited, for 'The Witch' by Mary Coleridge from her *Collected Poems*,
and for 'The Swans' and 'A Windy Day' by Andrew Young from his
Collected Poems; William Heinemann Ltd., for 'The Sea' by James
Reeves from *The Wandering Moon* and for 'Breathless' by Wilfrid
Noyce from *South Col*; David Higham Associates Ltd, for 'Inside'
and 'It Was Long Ago' by Eleanor Farjeon from *Silver Sand and Snow*
(published by Michael Joseph), and for 'The Death of Ned Kelly' by
John Manifold from his *Collected Poems*; Philip Hobsbaum, for 'With
Half an Eye'; Houghton Mifflin Company, for lines from 'Ombre
Chinoise' and 'September 1918' by Amy Lowell, for 'Charley Lee'
by Henry Herbert Knibbs from *Songs of the Lost Frontier* and for 'The
Walloping Window-Blind' by C. E. Carryl from *Davy and the Goblin*;
James Kirkup, for 'The Lonely Scarecrow'; Maxine Kumin, for 'The
Microscope', © 1963, by the Atlantic Monthly Company, Boston,
Mass.; Little, Brown & Co., for 'The Rhinoceros' by Ogden Nash;
J. B. Lippincott Company, for 'At the Dog Show' by Christopher
Morley; Miss Dorothea Mackellar, for 'Magic'; Macmillan & Co.
(and Mrs Iris Wise), for 'The Main Deep' by James Stephens from his
Collected Poems, and (with Mr Michael Gibson) for 'The Sweet-Tooth'
and 'When the Plane Dived' by Wilfrid Gibson from his *Collected
Poems 1905–1925*, for 'Colonel Fazackerley' by Charles Causley from
Figgie Hobbin and (with Mr M. B. Yeats), for 'The Cat and the Moon'

by W. B. Yeats from his Collected Poems; Macmillan London and Basingstoke, for 'Little Thomas' by F. Gwynne Evans from *Puffin, Puma and Co.*; The Macmillan Company (N. Y.), for 'On a Night of Snow' by Elizabeth Coatsworth from *Night and the Cat*; Eva Levy Marshall, for 'The Revolving Door' by Newman Levy from his *Gay But Wistful*; Meanjin Quarterly, for 'Wind' by Peter Miles; Melbourne University Press, for 'Invalid' by 'Furnley Maurice' from *The Bay and Padie Book*; Methuen & Co. Ltd., for 'Old Dan'l' by A. G. L. Strong from *The Body's Imperfection*, and (with Dr E. V. Rieu) for 'Sir Smasham Uppe'; Mrs Harold Monro, for 'Overheard on a Saltmarsh' by Harold Monro; William Morrow & Co. Inc., for extracts from *Stina, The Story of a Cook* by Herman Smith; John Murray (Publishers) Ltd., for 'Tim, an Irish Terrier' by Winifred Letts; Oxford University Press, for 'Song of the Sea Wind' by Austin Dobson, 'The Wife's Lament' by Nikolay Nekrasov (translated by Juliet M. Soskice) from *Who Can Be Happy and Free in Russia* (World's Classics Series) and for 'Seeds', 'Fireworks', 'The Old Wife and the Ghost', 'Mrs Button', 'Cows', 'The Ceremonial Band' and 'Miss Wing' by James Reeves from *The Blackbird in the Lilac*; Aileen and Helen Palmer, for 'The Road to Roma Jail' by Vance Palmer; Penguin Books, for 'The Door' by Miroslav Holub from *Selected Poems* translated by Ian Milner and George Theiner, © Miroslav Holub, 1967, translation © Penguin Books Ltd, 1967, and for 'Schoolmaster' by Yevtushenko from his *Selected Poems* translated by Robin Miller-Gulland and Peter Levi, S. J., © Robin Miller-Gulland and Peter Levi, 1962; The proprietors of *Punch*, for 'Noise' by Jessie Pope and 'The Vet' by Guy Boas; McGraw-Hill Ryerson Limited, for 'On the Way to the Mission' by D. C. Scott from his *Selected Poems* and for 'The Man Who Finds His Son Has Become a Thief' from *The Colour of the Times/Ten Elephants on Yonge Street* by Raymond Souster; Anthony Shiel Associates Limited, for 'Emperors of the Island' by Dannie Abse; The Society of Authors (as the literary representatives of the estate of John Masefield), for 'Spanish Waters', 'A Ballad of John Silver' and 'The Tarry Buccaneer' by John Masefield, and (with the literary trustees of Walter de la Mare), for 'The Little Creature', 'The Storm', 'Silver' and 'The Ride-by-Nights' by Walter de la Mare; Marguerite Steen, for extracts from *Little White King*; Douglas Stewart, for lines from 'Green Lions'.

While every effort has been made to trace copyright holders, in some cases this has not been possible. Should any infringement have occurred, the publishers tender their apologies.